BIG IDEAS
for Small
Mathematicians

Kids Discovering the Beauty of Math with 22 Ready-to-Go Activities

Ann Kajander

Zephyr Press

Chicago

The Library of Congress has cataloged the earlier edition as follows:
Kajander, Ann
     Big ideas for small mathematicians : kids discovering the beauty of math with 22 ready-to-go acvitities / Ann Kajander.
     p. cm.
Includes bibliographical references and index.
     ISBN 1-56976-155-8
1. Mathematics—Study and teaching (Elementary) 2. Mathematics—Study and teaching—Activity programs. 1. Title.
QA135.6.K35 2003
372.7—dc21   2002010805

Cover design: Monica Baziuk
Interior design: Dan Miedaner

© 2007 by Ann Kajander
All rights reserved
Published by Zephyr Press
An imprint of Chicago Review Press, Incorporated
814 North Franklin Street
Chicago, Illinois 60610
ISBN-13: 978-1-56976-213-4
ISBN-10: 1-56976-213-9
Printed in the United States of America
5 4 3 2 1

For Arthur, Robin, and Maria

Acknowledgments

Barb Kutcher had the original inspiration for the Kindermath Project, an enrichment project in elementary mathematics, for which these activities were designed. Since its inception, the project has been supported and encouraged by many members of the Canadian Mathematics Education Study Group. Ideas from members of this group—including George Kondor, Ralph Mason, Elaine Simmt, Brent Davis, Vicki Zack, and Bernard Hodgson—have inspired activities in this book.

Many elementary teachers as well as my students at Lakehead University have helped field test the ideas, particularly Colleen Modeland, Nicole Walter Rowan, Leila Desforges, Teena Bernardo, Joan Quequebush, and Suzanne Huot. I am also grateful for extensive help from Peter Taylor, translation help from Lori Ruberto, and help in disk preparation from Colleen Modeland.

My husband, Wally Drohan, was very supportive with his photography assistance, as well as sharing his office space for Kindermath classes. Colleagues who offered particular personal support have been Peter Taylor, Douglas McDougall, and George Gadanidis.

Contents

Introduction

Many children and adults believe mathematics to be a rather boring collection of difficult facts. Nothing is further from the truth! Learning mathematical facts in isolation is a bit like learning to spell but never reading or writing a story, or learning all about the technical skills of visual art but never creating a picture or examining the great works of other artists. Of course it would be boring to learn a subject this way.

It is just as possible to play with mathematical ideas before mastering the technical skills as it is to fingerpaint before learning about perspective and vanishing points. And creation is fun, even in math.

Practicing mathematicians find math to be exciting and fascinating. They love to play around and explore. In this book I have tried to collect some of the important ideas in mathematics that can be explored in a hands-on way. Some topics are a usual part of elementary school mathematics programs, such as activity 8 on tessellations or activity 10 on the number system, but I approach them in a new way. Some are topics not usually discussed with children, such as topology in activity 14. Nearly all of the topics are effective with older students as well. I have used

> *Learning mathematical facts in isolation is a bit like learning to spell but never reading or writing a story.*

many of the topics successfully with secondary-level students, and I often have to chase them out of the classroom when the bell rings!

These activities will work in a variety of situations:

- elementary classroom small-group problem-solving and exploration sessions
- math centers in the classroom
- math fairs
- special parent-and-child math days or evening sessions
- parent-and-child math exploration at home
- examples for mathematics teacher education

I know some elementary teachers who devote a period a week to mathematics exploration, and many parents are in search of engaging activities they can do with their children to stimulate their creativity and love of mathematics. The adult doesn't need a particular math background—all required background is supplied in the Mathematical Idea section of each activity.

Although the activity sheets can be used as is with children whose reading ability is sufficient, I prefer to deliver the instructions orally to children working in small groups. In this way, I can better control the pacing. One would hope that the next part of an activity would flow naturally from the students' questions. I find it is the interaction of the students with each other and with the adult that makes these activities richer. Often if children are led orally into answering questions and discussing the ideas while, say, they are making a tessellation, they don't even realize they are "talking math." Several of the activities can also be done in art class (such as activities 1, 6, 8, 9, 12, 21, and 22) or science class (activities 13 and 17), freeing up more time for investigation in math class.

The activities are roughly ordered from activities that all children can do to activities slightly better suited for children with a little more arithmetical skill, such as understanding the idea of multiplication. Within this ordering, activities are generally grouped by topic. The charts on pages ix–xi (Content Areas in Each Activity, Process Skills Used in Each Activity, and Prerequisite Knowledge and Skills for Particular Activities) detail the basic skills and topics of each activity as well as giving you an idea of what the children should know before embarking on a particular activity. That is not to say children cannot tackle a harder idea. I don't think it's always necessary to finish each activity or answer everything. Rather, the activities are meant to convey the idea that mathematics can be interesting, open-ended, uncertain, surprising, and highly creative.

Parents and teachers often think these ideas are only for bright kids. Given that the gifted are often underachieving, this may be a good use for the activities, but I have had surprising success using these activities with children branded as less skilled in mathematics. I remember a mother who came to me at wits' end with her fifth-grade daughter who hated mathematics and had poor technical

skills. When I spoke with her teacher, she told me the girl was "failing mathematics" and wondered "why the mother would send her to an enrichment program" (referring to the Kindermath program). This young lady managed to surprise everyone in the new environment. She discovered the trick to winning 3-D Tic Tac Toe (activity 20) in no time, and came up with a solution to the Streamers Problem (activity 19) on her own, which she shared with her class and her teacher. This experience changed her attitude toward mathematics and herself, and she gave learning the missing technical skills in school a much stronger effort. Three years later, I am told, she is now an A student in mathematics!

These activities are meant for exploration, enjoyment, and to stimulate curiosity. They can involve whole families in the wonder of mathematics. Enjoy the journey!

Many of the activities lend themselves to classrooms set up in groups.

How to Use This Book

Each activity in this book is divided into informative and instructional sections to make it easy to understand the ideas behind the activity as well as guide the students through the activity successfully.

- **The Big Idea:** This first section of each activity summarizes the underlying mathematical concept, so you can get the big picture before diving into the details.

- **Content Areas in This Activity:** This section lists the main mathematical content areas the activity involves. This information is also summed up for all activities in the chart on pages ix–x.

- **Process Skills Used in This Activity:** This section lists the main thinking and learning skills the students will use throughout the activity. This information is summed up for all activities in the chart on page xi.

- **Prerequisite Knowledge and Skills:** This section lists whether the children will need particular content knowledge before embarking on the activity. Most of the activities will be enjoyable for children on some level regardless of their previous knowledge and skills, but having these technical skills will make it easier for them to understand the math behind the activity. The chart on page xi lists this information for the activities as a whole.

- **Age Appropriateness:** Most of the activities in this book are suitable for all ages, with varying degrees of adult assistance. In this section, you will find suggestions for adapting various aspects of the activity to suit different age groups. For example,

younger children can often enjoy an activity without having to understand all of the mathematics behind it, but each activity is also set up to allow for further exploration of concepts as well as the introduction of terminology for older and more advanced students.

- **The Mathematical Idea:** This section describes the mathematical idea at the heart of the activity, to provide background for you and to assist you in following and facilitating the children's thinking. Often children have a correct but incomplete intuitive sense of a problem, and it is helpful for the adult to have a sense of the possible approaches to use.

- **Helpful Terms:** This box includes a list of terms relevant to the activity and their definitions. The purpose of this box is to enable you to review the basic terminology and concepts as well as to give you wording to use when explaining the ideas to the children. You will also find a complete glossary at the end of the book (page 138).

- **Making It Work:** This is the nuts-and-bolts section of the activity. Here you will find objectives, a list of materials you will need, preparation instructions, the activity procedure, suggestions for making the most of the activity and for helping the children through trouble spots, assessment ideas for determining if the activity was successful, and an extension activity or two for those kids who want to explore more.

- **Activity Sheet:** The activity sheet lists each step of the activity, as in the procedures section of Making It Work, but this sheet is directed to the children, with illustrations and hints to help them work through the activity successfully. For children able to read well and follow instructions, a photocopy of this activity sheet will assist you in taking them through each step, although this sheet is not meant to replace your active involvement and guidance. You may decide not to use the activity sheet for younger kids who won't be able to read it well, or if you prefer to take the class through the activity orally, without the help of written instructions.

> *The activities are meant to convey the idea that mathematics can be interesting, open-ended, uncertain, surprising, and highly creative.*

Content Areas in Each Activity

X = major idea in activity   * = idea included in activity   O = could optionally be included

Mathematical Topic	Activity Number																					
	1	2	3	4	5	6	7	8	9	10	11	12	13	14	15	16	17	18	19	20	21	22
Numeracy																						
addition, single digit		O								*						*	*	*	*			
subtraction, single digit																	*					
addition, double digit		O								*							*	*	*			
place value to 100										X												
multiplication, single digit		O				O	*										O	*	O			
division as partitioning											*											
division, single-digit divisor				O							O						O		O			
division with calculator						O					O											
equivalent fractions											X											
square numbers		O																*				
prime numbers						*																

(continued on next page)

Content Areas in Each Activity *(continued)*

X = major idea in activity   * = idea included in activity   O = could optionally be included

Mathematical Topic	Activity Number																					
	1	2	3	4	5	6	7	8	9	10	11	12	13	14	15	16	17	18	19	20	21	22
Measurement																						
areas of squares		*						*														
angles												*	O					*				
circles							X					*	O									
volumes					O													*			*	O
equivalent measures											*											
Patterning																						
geometric	X	*				*		*	*			*	*		*				O		*	*
numeric		*																*		O		
pattern rules	*	X						*											X		*	*
iterative patterns																		*			*	*
Geometry and Spatial Sense																						
3-D visualization			*	X	X									*	X				X		*	*
nets															X							
sketching in 3-D				O																		
terminology (geometric)			*	O	*	*	*									O		O				
intersections in space					*														*			
transformational geometry								X				X	O									
geometric recall											X											
fractal geometry																					*	*
Probability																						
sample space																X						
combinations																*						

Process Skills Used in Each Activity

X = major idea in activity   ***** = idea included in activity   **O** = could optionally be included

Process Skills	1	2	3	4	5	6	7	8	9	10	11	12	13	14	15	16	17	18	19	20	21	22
reasoning		*			*	*				*	*			*	*		*	*	*	*	O	
hypothesizing		*				O	*					*			*	O	*	X	*		O	O
problem solving					X		*			*	*			*	*	*	*	*	*	*	O	O
concept of proof		O							O								O	X	O		O	
communication	O	O	X							*									O			
creativity	*	*	*	*		*			*					*	*						O	
aesthetics of mathematics	*	*				*		*	*			*	*								*	*

Prerequisite Knowledge and Skills for Particular Activities

P = prerequisite   **H** = helpful

Prerequisites		2				6	7			10	11	12	13		15		17	18	19			22
previous activity		P											H									H
understanding of odd numbers		H																				
single-digit addition							P			P							P		P			
double-digit addition							P												P			
single-digit subtraction																	P		P			
single-digit multiplication (by hand or calculator)		H				H	H										H	P	H			
single-digit division (by hand or calculator)							H						H				H					
place value to 10										H												
fraction notation and meaning											P											
idea of area of squares																		P				
nets as surface area															H							

PATTERN SHAPES

The BIG Idea

Geometric patterns are the very essence of discovering new mathematical relationships.

Content Areas in This Activity
- Geometric patterning
- Pattern rules

Process Skills Used in This Activity
- Communication (optional)
- Creativity
- Aesthetics of mathematics

Prerequisite Knowledge and Skills
None

Age Appropriateness

This simple activity is appropriate for all ages.

The Mathematical Idea

Patterns are a central idea in mathematics. Almost anything that has a pattern contains some mathematics, and most mathematical ideas contain some rule or pattern. Recognizing increasingly subtle patterns is an important mathematical skill. This activity will introduce children to the concept of patterns, with an emphasis on enjoying their visual appeal. Showing examples of aesthetically pleasing patterns will enhance the activity and encourage children to be creative. Many quilts, for example, show remarkable patterns.

The central notion of a pattern is that it is predictable, once we see what is repeated. The pattern may change as we progress, but in a predictable way. Children should be able to identify what is repeated in their patterns, and what would come next. Patterns can be linear, nonlinear, or rotational. (See the box on page 2 for definitions of these terms.)

Wherever there is a pattern, there will be some math. Even if they can't yet name the patterns mathematically, children can still enjoy inventing them. Have fun creating!

HELPFUL TERMS

Patterns: Mathematical objects, such as numbers or shapes, that are continued in a predictable way are called *patterns*.

Geometric patterns: Patterns created using shapes are called *geometric patterns*.

Linear patterns: *Linear patterns* change by the same amount each time: for example, 2, 4, 6, 8, . . . (changing by 2) or red, blue, red, blue.

Nonlinear patterns: *Nonlinear patterns* change by a different amount each time: for example, 2, 4, 7, 11, 16, . . . (changing by 2, then 3, then 4, then 5, and so on) or red, blue, red, blue, blue, red, blue, blue, blue, . . .

Rotational patterns: *Rotational patterns* are patterns created by rotating a shape or image. For example, a minute hand traces a rotational pattern around a clock face.

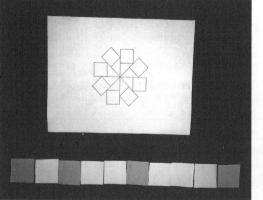

An important aspect of a pattern is that we can predict what would come next.

Pattern Shapes: Making It Work

Objectives

- Children will create geometric patterns.
- Children will connect the skills of pattern recognition, pattern creation, and spatial reasoning.
- The activity will encourage creativity and an aesthetic sense of mathematics.

Materials

✔ a few 8 ½" x 11" pieces of light cardboard or construction paper in several colors for each child

✔ scissors for each child

✔ glue stick for each child

✔ 11" x 17" piece of background paper for each child

✔ photographs of quilts and other geometric designs

✔ colored pens or pastels (unless using multicolored cardboard or paper)

✔ photocopy of the Pattern Shapes Activity Sheet (on page 5) for each child

☞ **T**ry cutting the shapes out of heavy wrapping paper or textured paper as well as cardboard. Alternatively, you could purchase pattern blocks, as shown in the photo on page 4.

Preparation

- You could speed up the process by creating shapes ahead of time. Copy and cut out the shapes on the activity sheet (on page 5). You can enlarge the shapes as desired. Trace them onto light cardboard or construction paper, cut them out, and color them (or use different colors of construction paper).

  Precut shapes in a variety of colors may help inspire children to be creative. You could even put together a few patterns as examples for the children.

Most children enjoy creating their own patterns from precut shapes.

- If you don't cut out the shapes ahead of time, make enough copies of the activity sheet for each child to have one.

- Enhance child creativity and comprehension by gathering photographs of quilts and other geometric designs.

👉 The book *Mathematical Quilts: No Sewing Required,* by Diana Venters and Elaine Krajenke Ellison (Emeryville, Calif: Curriculum Press, 1999), is a source of many wonderful ideas. The mathematics in each design allows for application at the secondary and even post-secondary levels. The Long Island Children's Museum website (www.licm.com) also has a hands-on quiltmaking feature. After entering the site, click on their hands-on activities and scroll down to the "QuiltMaker" link.

Procedure

1. Show children pictures of geometric patterns, such as quilts, to stimulate discussion and understanding of what a pattern is. Ask children what they think a pattern is and what it is not. Guide the discussion to include the idea that a pattern involves repetition.

2. Hand out the activity sheet (page 5), the background paper, glue sticks, cardboard or construction paper (and heavy wrapping paper or textured paper, if desired), and colored pens or pastels (unless using multicolored paper).

   If you precut the shapes, just hand out the shapes themselves. Give each child several of each shape so that everyone has plenty of shapes to choose from and can repeat shapes to form a pattern as desired.

3. Tell the children that they are to create any pattern they wish with the shapes. Encourage them to make a pattern, not just a pretty picture or set of random

shapes. They do not need to use all of the shapes. For example, a young child could simply make a checkerboard pattern with two colors of squares.

The pattern on the left contains both linear and rotational elements.

4. Choose questions to prompt children appropriately, depending on the situation. For example:

   • "How about a star?"

   • "In what other ways could you arrange the pieces?"

   • "Can you make this pattern repeat?"

   • "What would it look like if you made another ring of shapes?"

   • "Can you make your own quilt pattern?"

5. After they design patterns they like, children glue them onto their big piece of background paper.

Suggestions

   • Doing this activity in a group will encourage the children to share ideas.

   • Encourage children to be creative. Remember, math can be visual, creative, and just plain fun!

Assessment

Children are successful with this activity if they have created a clear pattern of their own.

Extension Activities

Children may enjoy making patterns on three-dimensional objects such as cardboard boxes. Another interesting challenge is to describe patterns using only words, so that someone else can create the same pattern. Children can try this in pairs, with another child whose pattern they haven't seen. Encourage simple explanations, stressing the idea of the repeated elements.

More fun with pattern shapes.

Pattern Shapes Activity Sheet

You can have a lot of fun making a pattern with even basic shapes, like the square, triangles, and parallelogram on the right.

1 Start by cutting out the pieces on the right (unless your teacher gives you other shapes to use).

2 Next, use these cut-out pieces to trace the shapes onto cardboard or construction paper. Trace a lot of them in various colors and cut them out. (If you trace onto plain cardboard or paper, use colored pens or pastels to color in the shapes.) You can cut out each shape in a single color (such as blue for your squares, red for one kind of triangle, green for the other, and so forth) or use several colors for each shape.

3 Now play with your pieces to make a design you like. Try to repeat the same pattern in your design.

4 When you have a pattern design you like, glue the pieces down on a big sheet of paper.

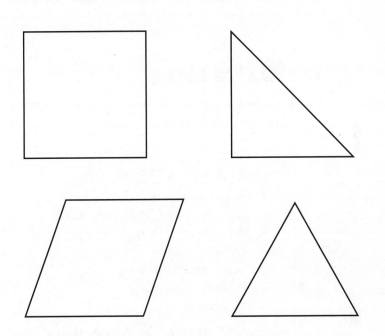

Cut out these pattern pieces and trace them onto cardboard, construction paper, wrapping paper, or textured paper.

SQUARES AND ODD NUMBERS

Activity 2

The BIG Idea

There is often a geometric illustration of a complicated idea that makes the idea easier to see.

Content Areas in This Activity

- Square numbers (optional)
- Addition, single digit (optional)
- Multiplication, single digit (optional)
- Areas of squares
- Geometric patterning
- Numeric patterning
- Pattern rules

Process Skills Used in This Activity

- Reasoning
- Hypothesizing
- Concept of proof (optional)
- Communication (optional)
- Creativity
- Aesthetics of mathematics

Prerequisite Knowledge and Skills

- Activity 1
- Understanding of odd numbers (helpful)
- Multiplication, single digit (helpful)

Age Appropriateness

Children as young as seven can appreciate this activity if they do it slowly. For very young children, stick to a geometric understanding of sizes of squares, rather than the more numeric concept of square numbers.

Mathematical Idea

Square numbers are easy to illustrate geometrically. They are simply the numbers that make actual square shapes. We can build a 2 x 2 square shape to illustrate the square number 4, a 3 x 3 shape to illustrate 9, and so forth. The first part of this activity involves using small cubes or tiles to build squares of various dimensions. This will illustrate the concept of a square number in a visual way.

The first square number: 1 x 1 = 1

The second square number: 2 x 2 = 4

The third square number: 3 x 3 = 9

The fourth square number: 4 x 4 = 16

The fifth square number: 5 x 5 = 25

The second part of the activity explores an interesting idea (called a *theorem*) about odd numbers and square numbers: If you add a list of odd numbers starting at 1, you always get a square number! For example, 1 + 3 + 5 = 9, so the sum of the first three odd numbers is 9. Here's another one: 1 + 3 + 5 + 7 + 9 = 25 so the sum of the first five odd numbers is 25. Geometrically (that is, by using actual shapes), we can build each new square number by adding another odd number.

We add the next odd number to our square to get the next square number. This square illustrates 1 + 3 + 5 + 7 + 9 = 25 (or a 5 x 5 square).

So we get the fifth square number (25) by adding the nine new cubes (or tiles) to the right of and below the 4 x 4 square—and 9 is the fifth odd number! We have a complicated-sounding mathematical theorem—the fact that the sum of the first n odd numbers is always n x n or n squared (n^2)—illustrated in something as simple as an array of squares.

HELPFUL TERMS

Area: *Area* is the number of 1 x 1 squares that it takes to cover a surface. For example, the area of a 2-inch by 3-inch rectangle is 6 square inches (that is, 2 x 3 = 6); in other words, it takes six 1-inch by 1-inch squares to cover it.

Even and odd numbers: *Even numbers* are divisible by 2, and *odd numbers* are not. Two people can share an even number of objects, but an odd number of objects will have one object left over.

Proof: A mathematical *proof* is a sequence of logical deductions to establish the truth of something new from something we know. If the proof applies to an idea that includes an infinite number of values, then examples are not enough to prove something, which is the case in this activity because odd numbers go on infinitely.

Square numbers: *Square numbers* represent the areas of squares that have sides of whole (not fractional) numbers. For example, 25 is a square number because it is the area of a 5 x 5 square. Simply, square numbers are the number of tiles (equal in size) needed to build a square.

Sum: *Sum* is a name for the number you get when you add two or more numbers. For example, the sum of 2 + 5 + 1 is equal to 8.

Theorem: *Theorem* is a name for a mathematical idea that can be proven always to be true.

Squares and Odd Numbers: Making It Work

Objectives

- Children will construct square numbers geometrically.
- Children will experience a first taste of a geometric proof by exploring the notion that if we keep adding the next odd number, we always get a square number.

Materials

- ✔ at least 25 small cubes, such as sugar cubes or centicubes, for each child (a variety of colors is ideal), or the same number of square tiles per child
- ✔ photocopy of the Squares and Odd Numbers Activity Sheet (on page 11) for each child

Preparation

None

Procedure 1: Building a Square

Older children who understand the concept of square numbers may want to skip to Procedure 2, opposite. You can focus on numerically defining square numbers through this first part of the activity, or you can simply define square numbers as the number of cubes (or tiles) needed to build a square, without explicitly listing all of the square numbers or getting into multiplication.

1. Hand out the activity sheet and cubes or tiles to each child. Have the children start with one cube (or tile). (If necessary, discuss the concept of 1 being a square number because the outline of one tile or one cube looks square; in other words, 1 x 1 = 1.)

2. Children should write down how many cubes it took to build the 1 x 1 square on the Square Numbers Chart (in the 1 x 1 row) on page 11.

3. Next, have the children construct a 2 x 2 square and record on the chart the number of cubes or tiles they used.

4. Repeat the process for a 3 x 3, 4 x 4, then 5 x 5 square.

5. Explain to the children that the number of cubes they use for each square is a *square number* because they can build a square out of that number of cubes.

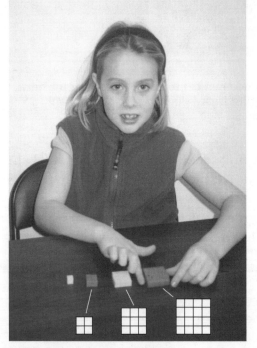

Building the square numbers.

Procedure 2: Adding Odd Numbers to Squares

This next part of the activity involves adding odd numbers to squares. You may need to review the concept of odd and even numbers with younger children before continuing.

1. Have children start with one cube or tile. Ask how many pieces they need to add to create a 2 x 2 square, then have them build it.

2. Ask how many pieces they need to add to the 2 x 2 square to create a 3 x 3 square, then have them build it.

3. At this point, ask the children if they notice anything special about the numbers they are adding to each square to make the next highest size. (They should recognize 3 and 5 as odd numbers.)

4. Next ask the children how many cubes are in their current squares (9). They started with 1 cube, added 3, then added 5 for a total of 9 cubes: 1 + 3 + 5 = 9. Do they notice a pattern here? Guide the discussion as necessary to the realization that adding successive odd numbers together, starting with 1, will always create a square number. (Older kids can take this further to the realization that 9 is the *third* square number and that they added *three* odd numbers together to get 9.)

5. Have the children continue adding odd numbers to their squares to create the next largest square. Ask them if they think the idea will always be true no matter how big the square. Could there ever be an example where it wouldn't work? What would it take to be sure it will always happen? You could introduce the terms *theorem* and *proof* this point.

6. Finally, ask them to show how they can separate their largest square into odd numbers again.

Historically, mathematicians required a formal algebraic argument to constitute a mathematical proof. More recently, with the increased use of computers, some mathematicians feel that geometric arguments, such as the one in this activity, although not considered a formal proof, should be given the status of a *dynamic proof*; that is, an argument based on visual, movable, geometric elements of a concrete nature to illustrate an idea in a convincing way. So sometimes even mathematicians aren't sure what a "good enough" argument is!

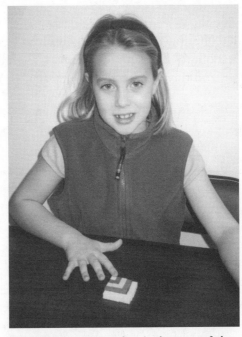

The fifth square number is the sum of the first five odd numbers.

Suggestions

- Building the squares with different colors—that is, using different colored cubes or tiles each time they add the next odd number—may make the idea clearer.

- Instead of handing out activity sheets and taking children through the above steps, you could pose the question: "Can you find a way to show that when you add up a list of odd numbers (starting with 1), you will always get a square number?" Allowing them to play with the idea is better than having them work through the directed activity, but of course this will work better with some children than with others.

Assessment

Determine understanding by asking the children to explain the ideas of squares and square numbers, as well as the ideas of proof and theorem, to the degree that you've discussed them.

Extension Activity

Have the children use other shapes to show that the idea works no matter what shapes you use to illustrate it, as long as you are using the same shape repeatedly (that is, you can't use triangles to build squares, for example). They could start with a triangle, then add three more triangles to make the next biggest triangle, as shown in the figure below.

If you start with one triangle, the second triangular shape is made from four triangles.

To get the next shape, they add the next odd number, or five triangles, to the bottom, giving the same sum as before—nine, or the third square number. Rectangles, diamonds, and other parallelograms will work too!

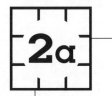

Squares and Odd Numbers
Activity Sheet

Discover a neat relationship between odd numbers and square numbers.

First let's learn about square numbers.

Part One _____

1 Start with one cube (or square tile). This will represent a 1 x 1 square. Write how many cubes (or tiles) are in this square in the Square Numbers chart (across from 1 x 1).

2 Next add pieces to build a 2 x 2 square. How many cubes (or tiles) are in this square? Write your answer across from 2 x 2 in the Square Numbers Chart.

3 Build a 3 x 3 square by adding to the 2 x 2 square and write the number of cubes (or tiles) in this square across from 3 x 3 in the Square Numbers Chart.

4 Add more pieces to the 3 x 3 square to build a 4 x 4 square and write the number of cubes (or tiles) in this square across from 4 x 4 in the Square Numbers Chart.

5 Add on again to build a 5 x 5 square and write the number of cubes (or tiles) in this square across from 5 x 5 in the Square Numbers Chart.

The new numbers in your chart (the number of cubes or tiles in each square) are called *square numbers* because we can build squares with them.

Square Numbers Chart

A square of this size . . .	requires this many cubes or tiles to build it (a square number):
1 x 1	_____
2 x 2	_____
3 x 3	_____
4 x 4	_____
5 x 5	_____

Squares and Odd Numbers
Activity Sheet

Part Two

1. Start with one cube (or tile) and build a 2 x 2 square. How many did you add to the one cube (or tile) to get a 2 x 2 square? _____

2. Now add cubes (or tiles) to your 2 x 2 square to build a 3 x 3 square. How many cubes (or tiles) did you add to get a 3 x 3 square? _____ Does this number have anything in common with the number you wrote in step 1?

3. How many cubes (or tiles) are in your current 3 x 3 square? _____

4. Try adding the next odd number (7) to your square. How many total cubes (or tiles) do you have now?

   _____

5. Keep adding odd numbers until you run out of cubes or tiles! Do you think you can keep getting bigger squares by adding an odd number?

6. Using your biggest square, show how you can separate it into odd numbers again.

Add new cubes (or tiles) to the right of and below the 2 x 2 square to create a 3 x 3 square.

Big Ideas for Small Mathematicians, 2007 © Zephyr Press

CUBES IN A ROOM

Activity

3

The **BIG** Idea

Verbally describing three-dimensional shapes requires careful communication.

Content Areas in This Activity
- Three-dimensional visualization
- Geometric terminology

Process Skills Used in This Activity
- Communication
- Creativity

Prerequisite Knowledge and Skills
None

Age Appropriateness

Children under the age of seven may have difficulty with this activity on their own, but most will be able to handle the activity with a grown-up such as a parent or older buddy observing and helping. Eight- to ten-year-olds should be able to work in pairs without a grown-up. In general, more intervention is needed with younger children to remind them that they must explain, not show or draw, the shape, and to help them select appropriate language.

Mathematical Idea

Communication is an important aspect of mathematical development. This activity encourages verbal communication, problem solving, and spatial reasoning. Children may develop an understanding of terminology such as *face, width, length, height, square, level,* and so forth as a natural outcome of this activity. They may also develop an appreciation of the need for precise mathematical language.

The activity involves creating a shape out of 27 or fewer cubes, a shape that must fit into the "room"—an open box that won't allow the shape to be larger than three cubes in any direction. After one child creates a shape, he or she must describe that shape using only words to a partner, who will try to reconstruct the shape based on the other child's words alone, without seeing the shape.

The child on the left is listening, asking, and building. The child on the right is describing.

HELPFUL TERMS

Cube: A three-dimensional object with six square faces is a *cube*. All the angles between edges are 90 degrees, or *right angles*.

Edge: An *edge* is the straight line that bounds a closed shape. For flat shapes, we usually call these *sides*, but in three dimensions we call them edges. For example, a cube has 12 edges—think of it as the number of toothpicks it would take to construct it.

Face: The flat outside surfaces of a three-dimensional solid are *faces*. For example, a cube has six faces.

Height: The vertical measure of an object, measured from the base to the highest point, is its *height*.

Length: *Length* is the measure of one dimension of a geometric object, such as one side of a rectangle.

Level: *Level* means flat or parallel to the floor, as in a balanced, or equally weighted, scale.

Square: A polygon (that is, a flat shape) with four equal sides is called a *square*.

Vertices: The point where two or more edges meet on a two- or three-dimensional shape is a *vertex*. For example, a triangle has three vertices, and a cube has eight vertices.

Width: The distance across a shape is its *width*.

Cubes in a Room: Making It Work

Objectives

- Children will improve their verbal communication skills in mathematics, possibly learning new mathematics terminology.
- Children will strengthen their ability to visualize in three dimensions.
- Children will build teamwork skills.

Materials

- ✔ 27 small cubes, such as sugar cubes or centicubes, for each child
- ✔ sheet of paper for each pair (two boxes can be made from an 8 ½" x 11" sheet)
- ✔ scissors
- ✔ transparent tape
- ✔ file folder or book (to hide shapes-in-progress from partner's view) for each pair
- 4 photocopy of Cubes in a Room Activity Sheet (page 17) for each child

Preparation

- Prepare the boxes ahead of time by first enlarging the template on page 15 to the size you need and making a photocopy for each child before cutting out the templates. This open-front paper box should be barely larger than the cube made with all 27 small cubes. This is the "room" for each structure.

    If your class will use centicubes, enlarge so that each square is about 1 ¼" x 1 ¼" (3.125 cm x 3.125 cm), making it slightly larger than the maximum size for the shape (which can't exceed 1 ⅕", or 3 cm, high or wide). If your class will use sugar cubes, measure a sugar cube, multiply that number by three, and add about ¼" (0.5 cm) to determine how big each square in the template should be.

- After you have photocopies of the template at the size you need, cut each one out and tape it into a box that will be open in the front and on the bottom. Double-check that the box is the right size for no larger than a three-cube by three-cube by three-cube structure.

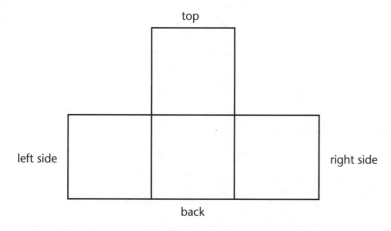

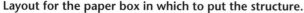

Layout for the paper box in which to put the structure.

Procedure

1. Have the children pair up, then explain that one of them will construct from the cubes a shape that must fit in the box. (You can tell them that it can't be bigger than three cubes in any direction, but often it is easier to explain by saying, "It must fit in the box.")

It is helpful to have the children practice building shapes before they build a shape to describe to their partners.

2. Have the children practice building shapes together at first to be sure the rules are clear: Shapes can be no bigger than three-cubes by three-cubes by three-cubes, and cubes must touch on edges or full faces. After completing a shape, each child should slide it into the box to make sure it fits.

☞ **A helpful way to demonstrate the idea is to build a cube out of all 27 cubes and then remove pieces to create a shape. Describing larger shapes can be too cumbersome and difficult for young children, so describing how to create the shape by removing pieces from a familiar shape may make this activity easier.**

3. After everyone understands the idea of creating the shape within size limits, have the children decide which of them will construct the shape first; then have them put up the divider between them.

4. The child who will build first makes a structure out of cubes as described above.

5. After finishing the structure, that child should slide it into the box to make sure it fits.

6. Then that child describes the shape orally so that the other can build it. Encourage the children to ask questions of the person who is describing the shape. Encourage the ones describing the shape to use correct mathematical terms, and not drawings or gestures. Discuss these terms as the need arises; for example, "We call the flat part a face."

7. After the children are able to duplicate their partners' shapes, repeat the process, but this time the other child in the pair creates and describes the shape.

Suggestions

- Children often think the idea is to have the others *not* guess their shapes. Emphasize that the idea is to describe their shapes well enough that the others can build it themselves.

- Sometimes with younger children (age eight or younger) it is helpful to suggest they describe the bottom layer first and be sure their partners understand before moving up to the second layer.

Assessment

Children can assess their own progress according to the accuracy of their partner's construction based on their instructions.

Extension Activities

For older children, remove the size restriction and allow them to build any shape they like, using as many cubes as they wish.

3 — Cubes in a Room Activity Sheet

Create a shape out of 27 (or fewer) cubes and describe it in words so that your partner can recreate the same shape without seeing it.

> If you're having trouble creating a shape that will fit your box, try creating a cube first, then pull pieces out to create your shape.

1 First choose a partner.

2 Next, both of you practice making shapes out of the 27 cubes. Each shape must be no bigger than three-cubes by three-cubes by three-cubes; in other words, it must fit in the box. Also, the cubes must touch on edges or full faces. Each time you create a shape, test its size by sliding it into the box. If it doesn't fit, re-create your shape so that it does.

3 Decide who will build first. Put up the divider so that your partner can't see what you create and create a new shape, still using no more than 27 cubes, following the same rules: The cubes must touch on edges or full faces, and the shape can't be larger than three-cubes by three-cubes by three-cubes— it must fit in the box.

4 Now describe your shape to your partner, who must try to build your shape using his or her own cubes. Use only words, not pictures or drawings. The other player may ask any questions he or she likes.

Remember, your goal is to describe your shape as clearly as possible using only words, so your partner can build it. You may find you need to use some new mathematical terms to make the job easier!

One possible shape.

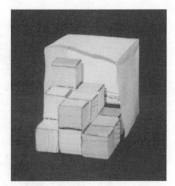

Testing the shape to be sure it fits in the box.

5 After your partner is able to build your shape, switch so that your partner describes a shape while you try to build it.

STRAW STRUCTURES

The **BIG** Idea

Three-dimensional objects are best seen in three dimensions—not two!

Content Areas in This Activity
- Three-dimensional visualization
- Geometric terminology (optional)
- Intersections in space

Process Skills Used in This Activity
Creativity

Prerequisite Knowledge and Skills
None

Age Appropriateness

Six-year-old children really enjoy making shapes. Older children may want to work on a shape of their own or the creation of particular assigned polyhedra.

Mathematical Idea

Three-dimensional objects often have faces composed of many two-dimensional shapes, such as squares, triangles, and parallelograms. This activity involves building a three-dimensional structure of any shape or design using straws and pipe cleaners. Through this exercise, the children can learn about many interesting properties of shapes. For example, the diagonals of squares need longer pieces than the sides when we are building them—an illustration of the Pythagorean theorem.

This is an activity for children to do together that is limited only by their creativity (and maybe their height!). It is simply fun to do in itself, but it is also a great opportunity to see different geometric shapes. Visualizing three-dimensional structures and shapes is hard to do on a two-dimensional page; working in three dimensions makes it easier to see the shapes.

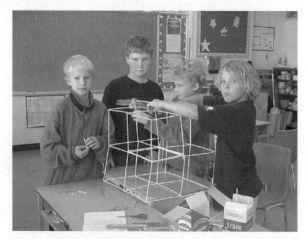

These fourth graders are working together to make a structure of cubes.

HELPFUL TERMS

Angle: The amount of rotation needed to get from one direction to another is an *angle*. Often we speak of the angle between two lines: This is the amount of rotation needed to get from one line to the other. It is often measured in degrees (see also *degree*).

Cube: A three-dimensional object with six square faces is a *cube*. All the angles are 90 degrees.

Degree: A unit for measuring rotation, abbreviated as °, is a *degree*. A complete rotation is said to be 360 degrees. This comes from the historical thought that it took 360 days for the Earth to revolve once around the sun. Two lines at right angles form angles of $^1/_4$ rotation, which is 90 degrees (that is, 360 divided by 4).

Diagonals: The lines drawn to connect opposite corners of a quadrilateral (four-sided) figure, or the lines connecting any vertex to any other nonadjacent vertex of a figure with more than four sides, are called *diagonals*.

Edge: An *edge* is the straight line that bounds a closed shape. For flat shapes, we usually call these *sides,* but in three dimensions we call them edges. For example, a cube has 12 edges—think of it as the number of toothpicks it would take to construct it.

Equilateral: A figure with all sides equal (which will make the angles equal, too) is *equilateral*. We refer to a triangle with all three sides equal as an equilateral triangle. We generally call an equilateral rectangle a square, so we don't really need the term equilateral in that context. For pentagons and shapes with more sides than that, the term *regular* is generally used to imply the sides are equal.

Face: The flat outside surfaces of a three-dimensional solid are called *faces*. For example, a cube has six faces.

Height: The vertical measure of an object, measured from the base to the highest point, is its *height*.

Hexagon: A shape with six sides is a *hexagon*. A regular hexagon is a shape with six equal sides.

Hypotenuse: This term specifically refers to the side of a right-angled triangle that is opposite the right angle—it will be the longest side of the triangle.

Length: *Length* is the measure of one dimension of a geometric object, such as one side of a rectangle.

Level: *Level* means flat or parallel to the floor, as in a balanced, or equally weighted, scale.

Parallelogram: A four-sided shape (quadrilateral) that has parallel opposite sides is a *parallelogram*. Opposite sides are also equal. A rectangle is a special parallelogram in which the angles are 90 degrees.

Pentagon: A flat geometric shape (polygon) with five sides is a *pentagon*.

Polygon: A flat (two-dimensional) shape with straight sides is a *polygon*. For example, a hexagon is a polygon with six sides. A *regular polygon* has all sides equal.

(continued on next page)

HELPFUL TERMS

Polyhedron: A *polyhedron* is a three-dimensional shape with polygons as faces. For example, a cube is a polyhedron with six square faces. The plural of polyhedron is *polyhedra*.

Pythagorean theorem: This theorem describes the relationship of squares drawn on each of the three sides of a right-angled triangle: The areas of the two smaller squares added together will always exactly equal the square drawn on the longer side (called the *hypotenuse*).

Regular and irregular: In polygons, a *regular* polygon means one with sides of equal length. So a square is a regular polygon, but a rectangle is not (unless it is a square). An *irregular* polygon is one with sides of unequal length.

Square: A polygon (that is, a flat shape) with four equal sides is called a *square*.

Tetrahedron: A three-dimensional shape (polyhedron) made with four triangular faces is a *tetrahedron*.

Three dimensional: A *three-dimensional* object isn't flat but uses up space (volume). For example, a square is two dimensional but a cube is three dimensional.

Triangle: A three-sided flat (plane) figure (or polygon) is a *triangle*.

Vertices: The point where two or more edges meet on a two- or three-dimensional shape is a *vertex*. For example, a triangle has three vertices, and a cube has eight vertices.

Width: The distance across a shape is its *width*.

Straw Structures: Making It Work

Objectives

- Children will have fun visualizing and creating their own three-dimensional shapes.
- Children will have the opportunity to learn geometric concepts, if not terminology, such as *face, edge, vertex,* and so on.
- Children will need to collaborate to create a shape together.

Materials

- ✔ straws (at least one package per group)
- ✔ pipe cleaners (one for every four straws)
- ✔ scissors for each small group
- ✔ glue stick for each small group
- ✔ ruler for each small group
- ✔ photocopy of Straw Structures Activity Sheet (on page 23) for each child or small group
- ✔ examples of geometric solids, such as a soccer ball (optional)

☞ **C**hildren can use balls of play clay (around ¹/₂ inch, or 1 cm) or even mini-marshmallows instead of pipe cleaners to form the joins.

Preparation

No preparation is necessary other than gathering the straws, pipe cleaners, and examples of geometric solids (if you wish), such as a soccer ball or photograph of a geodesic dome.

Procedure

1. Have the children get into small groups of up to four children and explain that they will be creating a structure using straws and pipe cleaners. You can ask them to build a specific shape of your choosing or allow them to build a structure of their choice. There are in fact a limited number of regular *polyhedra*—that is, three-dimensional objects that can be made out of a single geometric shape on the outside faces. Some models of geometric solids may be useful for inspiration. This is also the time to discuss terms such as *three dimensional* versus *two dimensional*, particularly noting that their three-dimensional structures will contain two-dimensional shapes. You could go over the various shape possibilities at this point. Be sure to emphasize that the structure must be a closed shape, meaning that you could enclose it by gluing paper on all outside faces.

2. Explain to the children the basics of joining the straws and pipe cleaners: First they should cut the pipe cleaners into about 6-inch (16-cm) pieces.

3. Next, they bend a pipe cleaner piece in half, then bend the ends in any direction they like. They should dab the ends with glue and insert each end into a straw, connecting two straws. They can also put glue on the folded end and insert that into a third straw, if they wish.

4. As a team, the children continue to join straws to form three-dimensional shapes. As they build, you can have conversations about the surfaces, edges (the straws), and vertices (the pipe cleaner joins) in the structure to help introduce or reinforce this terminology, giving students more ways to discuss their structures.

These fourth graders are proud of their structure, which contains many shapes.

Chapter 4

Suggestions

- Children may be surprised to discover that the diagonals of rectangular shapes are longer than the sides. They may not know it yet, but this is a hands-on experience with the Pythagorean theorem. You don't need to introduce this theorem (unless the kids are ready), but this property may warrant a rethinking of the design—to use edges cut shorter than one straw length, for example, so that a single straw can be used for a diagonal.

- It may also be fun to investigate the creation of large *polyhedra*. An adult working alongside the children might attempt to make a ball shape out of triangles, for example, and might ask, "Could we also make a big ball with just squares on the outside?" or "What other shapes can we use on the outside to make a big ball?" Props such as a soccer ball or photograph of a geodesic dome might be helpful here!

Assessment

For mathematical benefit, it is important that children do in fact make a three-dimensional closed shape out of the materials, not just any construction, such as a stick man. Comparing the results to existing solid objects may help children assess their own success.

Extension Activity

Children who have created a particular polyhedron may want to cover the outside surface area with pieces of tissue paper or other light paper to create the effect of a geometric solid. The pieces should be cut to the size of each exterior facet and glued to the straws forming the edges. The volume of the solid would be the space trapped inside by the faces, and the surface area would be the amount of paper used.

Straw Structures
Activity Sheet

4

Using straws and pipe cleaners, you and your friends can create some great three-dimensional structures. These three-dimensional structures can be formed from many familiar two-dimensional shapes.

1 First, get into small groups and prepare the pipe cleaners by cutting them into about 6-inch (16-cm) pieces.

2 To begin connecting straws, bend a pipe cleaner piece in half, then bend the ends in any direction you like. Dab the ends with glue and insert each end in a straw, connecting two straws. (You can also put glue on the folded end and insert that into a third straw, if you wish.)

3 Now you're ready to start building your structure. If you can't think of what to make, start with a simple cube. Then think of what to add to it. Can you make an archway big enough to walk through? Or a building, or a bridge? How about a huge cube made of a lot of smaller cubes? Or a large dome shape?

4 When you're done, see how many geometric shapes you can find in your structure!

SOMA CUBES

Activity
5

The **BIG** Idea

Seven different arrangements of four or fewer cubes fit together to make a larger cube. Someone invented this in his head!

Content Areas in This Activity
- Three-dimensional visualization
- Volumes (optional)
- Sketching in three dimensions (optional)
- Geometric terminology

Process Skills Used in This Activity
- Reasoning
- Problem solving

Prerequisite Knowledge and Skills
  None

Age Appropriateness

This activity is suitable for all ages. Eight- to ten-year-olds will be able to find most of the individual pieces necessary on their own, except possibly the harder two shown on page 25.

The Mathematical Idea

A Danish writer named Piet Hein, while attending a lecture on quantum physics by Werner Heisenberg, had the idea that all the irregular shapes made with four or fewer cubes would themselves form a cube when put together. After the lecture he confirmed his idea.

This activity explores Hein's ideas by having children build the six possible irregular shapes made from four cubes, plus the one irregular shape made from three cubes. These shapes are called *soma cubes*.

Only three cubes

The seven soma pieces—irregular shapes made out of four or fewer cubes.

First children will make the two possible regular shapes out of four cubes (as shown in the illustration on page 27). They do this to aid their understanding of regular versus irregular. Then children make the one irregular shape using three cubes (as shown in the photo on page 24) and six different irregular shapes using four cubes.

Building and gluing the soma pieces.

At last! Fitting all seven soma pieces together into a cube.

The next step in the activity, after building the seven irregular shapes, is to build a 3 x 3 x 3 cube out of the seven shapes. So children need 24 cubes in all to make the six irregular shapes of four cubes, plus three cubes for the three-cube irregular shape (as shown in the photograph on page 24): 27 cubes in all to construct the seven shapes. Note that the 3 x 3 x 3 cube they create from these shapes must indeed contain 27 cubes.

It is tempting to think that two identical pieces that are positioned differently on the table are not the same pieces. This activity is good not just for problem solving, but to work on spatial reasoning in three dimensions (that is, three-dimensional visualization). Understanding and using transformational geometry (such as the ideas of reflection and rotation) may help children see that two pieces that look different may be the same. For example, we might flip one over and see that it is identical to another piece.

The two most difficult to construct pieces are shown in the photo at right. Although these two pieces look like mirror images of each other, one, in fact, cannot be derived by moving the other around. They are two different pieces.

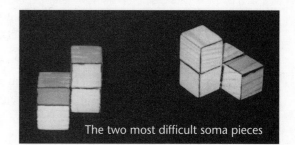

The two most difficult soma pieces

The art of soma has fascinated hobbyists for some time, and many interesting arrangements other than a cube are possible with the seven pieces. After the children finish with this activity, they can have fun exploring the many possible arrangements of the soma pieces.

HELPFUL TERMS

Cube: A three-dimensional object with six square faces is a *cube*. All the angles are 90 degrees.

Face: The flat outside surfaces of a three-dimensional solid are called *faces*. For example, a cube has six faces.

Reflection: Literally, a *reflection* is what you see when you look in a mirror, or the "mirror image" of something. In transformational geometry, reflection involves flipping an object, often to see if it looks the same (or the opposite) when flipped.

Regular and irregular: In polygons, a *regular* polygon means one with sides of equal length. So a square is a regular polygon, but a rectangle is not (unless it is a square rectangle). An *irregular* polygon is one with sides of unequal length.

In this activity, the arrangements of four cubes that are symmetrical are called regular arrangements. That is, the cubes are arranged in a square or in a row that when divided in half form two identical halves. The arrangements that are not symmetrical are called irregular arrangements.

Rotation: When you move (or turn) an object in a circular path around a point called the center, you are *rotating* the object. For example, the tip of a clock hand rotates around the center of the clock; it follows a rotational pattern. In this activity, children can rotate their shapes to see if, after turning, the shapes resemble other shapes.

Three dimensional: A *three-dimensional* object isn't flat but uses up space (volume). For example, a square is two dimensional but a cube is three dimensional.

Transformational geometry: The geometry of moving shapes around. For example, translations (slides), rotations (turns), and reflections (flips) are movements that are possible in *transformational geometry*.

Translation: Also known as sliding, *translation* means moving an object from one position to another in a straight-line movement.

Soma Cubes: Making It Work

Objectives

- Children will practice visualizing geometric shapes in three dimensions.
- Children will practice problem solving with these three-dimensional geometric shapes.
- Children will learn the difference between regular and irregular, and may encounter geometric terms such as rotation, translation, reflection, and face.

Materials

- ✔ 35 small cubes, such as sugar cubes or centicubes, for each child
- ✔ glue for each child or small group
- ✔ photocopy of the Soma Cubes Activity Sheet (on page 29) for each child
- ✔ extra cubes, in case of mistakes (approximately four for each child)

Preparation

None

Procedure

1. Discuss the difference between an irregular geometric shape and a regular one, introducing or reviewing the concept of symmetry as well as terms such as face and edge.

2. Tell the children they will first build two regular arrangements of four cubes (as shown in the illustration at right-top). Before they begin, however, they will need to understand the most important rule: Cubes must touch at least one other cube on a full face. Otherwise there would be an infinite number of arrangements.

3. Guide them as necessary. You may want to build an example out of cubes or show the illustration below to younger kids.

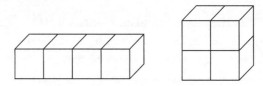

Two regular arrangements of four cubes.

4. Next, children will make an irregular shape, the only irregular shape they can make using three of the cubes. Build a model or show the illustration below to help younger children.

The only irregular arrangement of three cubes.

5. Children then will make the only six irregular shapes one can make using four cubes for each shape. Children need to understand that the six shapes they are looking for do not include the two regular shapes they made in step 2.

6. Each time they create an irregular shape from four cubes, they should glue the cubes together.

Encourage children to pick up a newly assembled piece and play with it. If there is no way of moving it to make it look like an existing piece, it probably isn't. This is a good time to introduce terms like reflection (flip), translation (slide), and rotation (turn).

7. After they have found and glued all seven pieces (the one three-cube arrangement, and the six with four cubes), it is time to start the real fun—assembling them into a 3 x 3 x 3 cube. Children may be surprisingly fast at this. (Grown-ups with less patience can refer to the photographs to follow!)

Suggestions

- This activity is terrific for an adult and child to do together, especially when making the finished cube. Children are often very good at spatial reasoning, and the child may figure it out sooner than the adult, making it a good confidence builder for the child (and amusing, or frustrating, for the adult!).

- Finding all six irregular shapes and then building a cube may take some members of the group quite a while. To avoid frustration, encourage those who do find the solutions to share with those who are having trouble.

Assessment

Children are successful if they can demonstrate understanding of irregular and regular shapes by creating all shapes in this activity, and if they can demonstrate three-dimensional visualization skills by creating the cube. Children get very excited when they successfully assemble the cube.

Extension Activity

Have children try drawing the seven soma shapes on isometric dot paper to sharpen their abilities to visualize in three dimensions by sketching in three dimensions.

Beginning to assemble the cube out of the seven soma pieces.

The partially assembled cube.

The finished cube made with the seven soma pieces.

Soma Cubes Activity Sheet

Visualizing in three dimensions is an important math skill. In this activity, you get to build regular and irregular shapes using cubes (which are three-dimensional shapes).

1 There are two ways to arrange four cubes into a regular shape so that they touch on at least one full face each. Can you create these two shapes of four cubes each?

> These are called regular arrangements because they are so *symmetric*—if you divide the shapes in half (horizontally or vertically) with a straight line, each half will look the same.

2 Next, build an irregular shape, this time using only three cubes. You can make only one irregular shape out of three cubes. As in step 1, be sure that the cubes touch another cube on at least one full face.

3 When you've found the shape, glue the three cubes together. (Check with your teacher before gluing if you're not sure you have the right shape.)

4 Now try to find the six irregular shapes made from four cubes. When you find an arrangement, glue the four cubes together.

> To check if you have found a new arrangement, pick up your new shape and turn it all around and upside down. If it still doesn't look like any of the other arrangements you've found, it must be a new shape.

5 Now that you have found all six irregular arrangements of four cubes, and the one irregular arrangement of three cubes, you will notice you have used 27 cubes in all. It turns out these shapes will fit together to make all sorts of interesting things . . . including a 3 x 3 x 3 cube! Fitting the pieces together may drive you and your friends crazy for quite a while. The finished cube is called a *soma cube*.

6 After you've figured out how to fit all of the pieces into a cube, you can have fun making all sorts of different shapes. See how many you can find!

DIVISIBILITY CIRCLE 6

The **BIG** Idea

Some numbers can be divided exactly by other numbers and some can't.

Content Areas in This Activity

- Multiplication, single digit (optional)
- Division, single-digit divisor (optional)
- Prime numbers
- Geometric patterning
- Geometric terminology

Process Skills Used in This Activity

- Reasoning
- Hypothesizing (optional)
- Creativity
- Aesthetics of mathematics

Prerequisite Knowledge and Skills

- Multiplication, single digit (helpful)

Age Appropriateness

Children of nearly any age will enjoy making patterns with the yarn. After about age seven, they can start to see the products of numbers in the regular polygons: For example, they can see that a square created on a divisibility circle with 12 notches is four sides of three units, and four groups of three is 12, or 4 x 3 = 12. Children from age eight or nine may be able to see the result of the numbers that divide evenly into 12, those that don't divide evenly, and why.

Mathematical Idea

Some numbers can be divided exactly by other numbers. For example, 12 is divisible by 2, 3, 4, and 6. Some numbers, like 5 and 7, can only be divided by 1 and themselves. These are called *prime numbers*. The numbers that divide exactly into a given number are called *factors*. The number 12, for example, has a lot of factors: 2, 3, 4, and 6 all divide evenly into 12, and so they are called the *factors of 12*.

This activity illustrates the above concept of divisibility geometrically. If we make a 12-notched divisibility circle, and wind the yarn around every fourth notch, we make an equilateral triangle (all the sides have the same length). If we wind it every second notch, we will have a hexagon (see the illustration on page 31). All these numbers (3 and 4, as in the three sides of the triangle wrapped around every fourth notch, and 6 and 2, as in the six sides of the hexagon wrapped around every second notch) are factors of 12.

If we wind the yarn by a number of units such as 5, which does not divide exactly into 12, it will not make a regular (all sides equal) polygon, but it will make some other interesting shapes, such as star shapes, if we keep winding!

Divisibility circles can also be made with other numbers of notches, but beware: If you choose a prime number like 7 or 11, you will only be able to form the regular polygon with that number of sides.

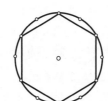

The hexagon has six sides, each of which is two units long.

HELPFUL TERMS

Composite number: A number that has whole number factors is a *composite number*; in other words, it has numbers that divide into it with zero remainder other than 1 and itself. Numbers that do not have such factors are *prime*. For example, 6 is composite because it can be divided by 2 and 3, with zero remainder. *Note:* By convention, 1 is considered to be neither prime nor composite.

Diameter: The distance across a circle, through the center, is called the *diameter*.

Divisibility: The *divisibility* of a number describes whether any numbers can be divided into it with no remainder. For example, 10, 15, and 20 are divisible by 5. The divisibility rule for 5 is that 5 will divide evenly (with no remainder) into numbers that end in 5 or 0.

Equilateral: A figure with all sides equal (which will make the angles equal, too) is *equilateral*. We refer to a triangle with all three sides equal as an equilateral triangle. We generally call an equilateral rectangle a square, so we don't really need the term equilateral in that context. For pentagons and shapes with more sides than that, the term *regular* is generally used to imply the sides are equal.

Factors: Numbers that divide evenly (with no remainder) into a number are *factors* of that number.

Hexagon: A shape with six sides is a *hexagon*. A regular hexagon is a shape with six equal sides.

Pentagon: A flat geometric shape (polygon) with five sides is a *pentagon*.

Polygon: A flat (two-dimensional) shape with straight sides is a *polygon*. For example, a hexagon is a polygon with six sides.

Prime number: A number that has no factors other than itself and 1 is a *prime number*. That is, it can't be divided evenly (with no remainder) by numbers other than itself and 1. For example, 5 is prime because 5 = 1 x 5 only, but 6 is not prime because 6 = 2 x 3 as well as 1 x 6.

Product: The result we get when multiplying two or more numbers is called a *product*. For example, multiplying 2 times 3 gives a product of 6.

Regular and irregular: In polygons, a *regular* polygon means one with sides of equal length. So a square is a regular polygon, but a rectangle is not (unless it is a square rectangle). An *irregular* polygon is one with sides of unequal length.

Square: A polygon (that is, a flat shape) with four equal sides is called a *square*.

Triangle: A three-sided flat (plane) figure (or polygon) is called a *triangle*.

Chapter 6

Divisibility Circle: Making It Work

Objectives

- Children will connect the idea of factors to a geometric image.
- Children will play with number combinations in a geometric way.
- Children will enjoy creating mathematical patterns.

Materials

- ✔ circle cut out of cardboard, about 8" (20 cm) in diameter, for each child
- ✔ circular object, such as a coffee can (optional)
- ✔ 6' to 8' (about 2 to 2.5 m) bright yarn (or string) per child
- ✔ tape for each child or small group
- ✔ adult scissors to poke a hole through the cardboard center
- ✔ scissors for each child or small group
- ✔ a clock face that's slightly larger than the circle (optional)
- ✔ photocopy of Divisibility Circle Activity Sheet (page 34) for each child

Preparation

- Prepare the cardboard circles (with an 8-inch, or 20-cm, diameter) for each child. You can use a circular object, such as a coffee can base, as a template for tracing the circle.
- For younger children, precut the notches as well. You can cut the 12 notches evenly around the perimeter by laying the cardboard down over a clock face. Alternatively, you could fold a paper circle into quarters, then continue to fold the quarter-circle into thirds. When you open the paper, you will have 12 fairly evenly spaced folds. You can then use this as a template for cutting the 12 notches. If you cut the notches in a V shape, the children can wrap the yarn around the back to get to the next notch. Or you could cut each notch as two side-by-side slits.
- Using adult scissors, poke a hole in the center of each circle, through which the children can thread the yarn and knot it or tape it in place.
- Cut the yarn or string into pieces 6 to 8 feet (about 2 to 2.5 m) long for each child.

Procedure

1. If you haven't precut the notches, have the children do so, taking turns using the clock face or paper circle (described above) as a template for where the notches should go.

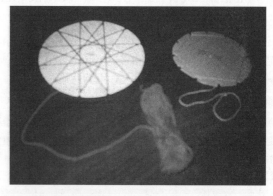

Stars and hexagons are just a few of the possible shapes children can create.

2. Then each child threads the yarn (or string) through the hole, knotting it or taping it down to the back of the circle.

3. Encourage the children just to play with the circle at first. They may soon notice that they can make interesting patterns. Children may need a little help initially to see how to wrap the yarn around the back to the next notch, then through that to the front again, so it will outline a shape on the circle.

4. Once children understand how to create shape outlines, ask them to make specific shapes, such as a square, an equilateral triangle, or a regular hexagon (introduce terminology as needed). Ask older children if they can make a five-sided figure (a regular pentagon), and encourage them to think about why not. This is a good environment to talk about products, factors, divisibility, and even prime numbers for children in fourth or fifth grade.

Children can experiment with all kinds of shapes using their divisibility circles.

Suggestions

All children can enjoy exploring other shapes, too, such as stars.

Assessment

Looking at the shapes produced will provide a visual assessment. For older children, the activity could be tied in to a look at factors and divisibility. Assess their comprehension of these concepts and their ability to use the terminology correctly with the use of the divisibility circle.

Extension Activity

Children can make divisibility circles with other numbers of notches. For example, what shapes can they make with a circle of nine notches? Ask the children if they make a divisibility circle with a different number of notches, would they be able to make as many polygons? Why or why not? If they make one with 11 notches, which regular polygons (square, hexagon, and so forth) could they make? Encourage exploration of prime and composite numbers for as long as it is fun!

Divisibility Circle Activity Sheet

6

With a divisibility circle, you can make interesting patterns and investigate some mathematics too, particularly geometric shapes.

1 If your teacher hasn't already done so, cut 12 evenly spaced notches in your circle. A clock face is a helpful model for where to place each notch.

2 Next, poke a hole in the center of your circle and thread the piece of yarn through it. Knot the yarn or tape it down on the back of the circle.

3 Try to make some geometric shapes by wrapping the yarn around the notches, from front to back to front again, to make the sides of shapes. For example, you can make a square by wrapping the yarn around every third notch, or an equilateral triangle by wrapping it around every fourth notch.

An *equilateral triangle* is a triangle with sides that are all the same length. Other shapes with sides of the same length are called *regular polygons*.

4 Can you make a six-sided figure, a hexagon, with all sides equal? Can you predict whether you could make a pentagon with all five sides the same length? Why or why not?

5 Have fun investigating polygons and then try making some star shapes.

Big Ideas for Small Mathematicians, 2007 © Zephyr Press

DISCOVERING PI

The **BIG** Idea

There is a relationship between the diameter and circumference of all circles: We call it *pi*.

Content Areas in This Activity
- Multiplication, single digit
- Division with calculator (optional)
- Circle measurement
- Geometric terminology

Process Skills Used in This Activity
- Hypothesizing (optional)
- Problem solving
- Concept of proof (optional)

Prerequisite Knowledge and Skills
- Addition, single digit
- Addition, double digit
- Multiplication, single digit (helpful)
- Division, single digit (helpful)

Age Appropriateness

Children will find the direct relationship harder to discover if they are not familiar with multiplication. Eight-year-olds are sometimes able to think about multiplication by three as "three groups of something." Younger children may be able to see the "add six" relationship in the first part of the activity, and the "add up the diameter three times" in the second part of the activity, but they may not be able to connect the two.

Children need to be familiar with division for the second extension activity of calculating pi more accurately.

Mathematical Idea

There is a relationship between the diameter of a circle and the distance around it, the *circumference*: C = pi x D. As the diameter increases by 1, the circumference will increase by slightly more than 3, or the number pi. The actual number pi represents is 3.14159 . . . with the decimal places going on forever. We use the Greek letter π to symbolize pi. Children can discover an approximation of this relationship themselves with this two-part activity.

In the first part, children create rings of pennies to discover that with each new ring, they add two pennies to the diameter and six pennies to the circumference (which is three times the number of pennies added to the diameter). Children can make a chart to find out that each new ring always adds three times as many pennies to the circumference as to the diameter.

They can also have fun measuring other circles to verify the idea in the second part of this activity. Circles on the playground are ideal, but you can also create circles with chalk on the floor or use the circles that may already exist on a gym floor. The bigger the diameters and circumferences of the circles, the more accurate the results will be. The diameter will always be just over three times the circumference.

Measuring the diameter using string—your students will try this with much larger circles.

The circumference will be about three times as long as the diameter.

HELPFUL TERMS

Circumference: The perimeter of, or distance around, a circle is called its *circumference*.

Diameter: The distance across a circle, through the center, is called the *diameter*.

Pi: This is the name for a special number (3.14159 . . .), written using the Greek letter π, that is the number of times you have to multiply the diameter of a circle to get the circumference. Pi's decimal expansion goes on forever.

Product: The result we get when multiplying two or more numbers is called a *product*. For example, multiplying 2 times 3 gives a product of 6.

Discovering Pi: Making It Work

Objectives

- Children will discover the relationship between diameters and circumferences of circles.
- Children will construct an approximation of the number pi.

Materials

- ✔ about 40 pennies or small circular disks for each child
- ✔ string for each child (how long depends on the size of the circles you choose to have children measure)
- ✔ calculator for each child or small group
- ✔ scissors for each child
- ✔ yard stick (or meter stick) for each child or small group
- ✔ chalk or masking tape (optional)
- ✔ photocopy of Discovering Pi Activity Sheet (pages 40–41) for each child

Preparation

Choose (and create, if necessary) what circles to have the children measure for the second part of the activity. You can use circles already drawn on the playground or gym floor, or use chalk to trace around a circular object, such as a garbage can.

> **☞** **C**hildren may need to build the first penny ring with an adult. It may be helpful to mark the center penny in some way, such as with a small object on top, to help keep the construction clear when the rings get large.

Procedure 1: Penny Circle

The two parts of this activity can be done one after the other or at different times.

1. Start with the penny circle by having the children put one penny in front of them and then create a circle around this penny.

The first ring of pennies.

2. Discuss the concepts of *diameter* and *circumference* so that children understand the idea, if not the actual terminology, of how many pennies go across the circle versus how many pennies go around.

3. Next have the children add a ring of pennies around the first ring so that the pennies in both rings touch. How many did they add to the diameter with this second ring? This number is already recorded on the Penny Circles Chart (page 41) on their activity sheets to get them started.

4. Now have them count how many pennies are in the second ring (that is, how many pennies make up the circumference of the second ring). Ask them how many more pennies are in this ring than in their first ring. Have them record this number on the chart on their activity sheet, next to Ring 2, under "Pennies added to circumference." They should record "+6" because the first ring has six pennies and the second ring should have 12.

5. Have them repeat the process by adding more rings of pennies, each time counting how many pennies they added to the diameter and to the circumference, recording both numbers in the chart. The chart is set up to record five rings, but building three or four rings should be enough to see the "+2 across, +6 around" pattern.

Children will enjoy counting and recording the number of pennies in the rings. They will soon see that the number in the ring goes up by six each time. They need to be encouraged, however, to relate this to the increase in the diameter. Remind them that adding a new ring adds two pennies to the diameter. So if the diameter goes up by two, the circumference goes up by three times that much, or six.

Procedure 2: Large Circles

The next part of this activity involves measuring the diameters and circumferences of large circles, on the playground or on the gym or classroom floor. The larger the circles you choose, the more accurate the measurements will be.

1. Have each child use a yard stick (or meter stick) to measure the diameter of the first circle you've chosen and record this on the Large Circles Chart (page 41) on their activity sheets.

Children unable to multiply should be directed to measure the diameter first using string instead of the yard (or meter) stick, and then see how many of those lengths are needed to go around the circle. It should be about three of the diameter lengths. Using this method eliminates the need to measure the string at all.

2. Next they use string to measure the circumference of the circle. Each child wraps the string around the circle and cuts it to size. Then the child can measure the string using the yard stick and record the measurement in the circumference column for the first circle on the Large Circles Chart.

Depending on the children's age, you can explain the number three further as the special number pi, discovered long ago by geometers but still fascinating to mathematicians. This could also be a time to introduce the idea of "going on forever" as the digits of pi do.

3. After they measure the first circle or two, have them measure just the diameter of a third circle and see if they can guess what the circumference will be. Older children will be able to use a calculator with assistance to find out a good approximation of the ratio of diameter to circumference. The Large Circles Chart is set up for five circles, but of course your class can do more or fewer depending on how quickly they pick up on the diameter-circumference relationship. Alternatively, each group can do one circle, then all groups can share their measurements on the board.

4. Once they see the relationship between the diameter and the circumference, ask if they think that relationship will be true for all circles. Can they think of something else circular they could apply this new idea to, measuring just the diameter or just the circumference and figuring out the other?

Suggestions

- It may be helpful to leave the penny circles for a while and go on to the next part of the activity, then come back to the pennies. The larger circles of the second part of the activity will give more accurate results. Often a child will then notice that the diameter-circumference relationship is the same as in the first part of the activity.

- Constructing chalk circles on the floor with diameters of whole numbers of units, such as 1 yard or 1 meter, will make the result clear for children just learning to multiply.

Assessment

Children can explain the diameter-circumference relationship to a peer or an adult. They can predict the approximate circle circumference for a given diameter.

Extension Activities

- Ask children, "If you knew the diameter of the Earth, how could you find the distance around the world at the equator?"

- Discuss with children that although it may seem that the circumference is always three times the diameter, the actual number is an endless decimal number that starts with 3.14159. Mathematicians named it *pi* after one of the Greek letters, a long time ago (we use the Greek letter π for it). Ask the children to see how accurately they can calculate pi by measuring the diameter and circumference of a very large circle carefully. Hint: If $C = \pi \times D$ then $C \div D = \pi$

Here are two different activities involving circles that will help you discover the mathematical relationship between the distance across a circle and the distance around a circle.

Penny Circles _____

1 Start with one penny in front of you, then make a ring of pennies around that one. Your ring should have six pennies in it. These pennies are the *circumference* of the circle (the distance around it).

2 Now make a second ring of pennies around that first ring. Count how many pennies you *added* to the diameter (to the number of pennies going across). Remember that adding a new ring adds one penny to each side. Check that the answer you got is the same as what is already filled in in your Penny Circles Chart.

3 Next count how many pennies are in the second ring. How many more pennies are in this ring than are in the first ring? Write this number in "Pennies added to circumference" column in the Penny Circles Chart (next to the "+2"). What do you predict will happen if you make a third ring of pennies? How many pennies will you add to the diameter? How many will you add to the circumference?

4 Add another ring of pennies and count how many pennies you *added* to the diameter and write this in the "Pennies added to diameter" column in the Ring 3 row.

5 Count how many pennies you *added* to the circumference and write this in the "Pennies added to circumference" column for Ring 3.

6 Continue building rings and filling in the chart until your teacher tells you to stop. Can you make a prediction about the relationship between the amount the diameter increases and the amount the circumference increases? Do you think they are related?

Large Circles _____

1 For this part of the activity, you will be measuring a few large circles. Use a yard or meter stick to measure the distance across the circle (diameter). Record this in the Large Circles Chart, in the "Diameter" column for Circle 1.

2 Next use string to measure the distance around the circle (circumference). Do this by laying out the string exactly along the circle's edge, cutting the string once you've gotten back to the beginning. Then measure the string. Write this measurement in the "Circumference" column for Circle 1.

3 Now measure a second circle, starting with the diameter. Can you predict how big the circumference will be if you know the diameter? (Use a calculator to help you if you like.)

Do you think the same relationship will hold for all circles? Can you think of an example of something circular you could measure using your idea? Continue measuring any circles your teacher provides, recording your measurements on the chart.

Big Ideas for Small Mathematicians, 2007 © Zephyr Press

Discovering Pi Activity Sheet

Penny Circles Chart		
	Pennies added to diameter	Pennies added to circumference
Ring 2	+2	
Ring 3		
Ring 4		
Ring 5		

Large Circles Chart		
	Diameter	Circumference
Circle 1		
Circle 2		
Circle 3		
Circle 4		
Circle 5		

TESSELLATIONS

Activity **8**

The **BIG** Idea

Tiles completely covering the floor can have lots of shapes. Just ask Escher!

Content Areas in This Activity

- Areas of squares
- Geometric patterning
- Pattern rules
- Transformational geometry

Process Skills Used in This Activity

- Creativity
- Aesthetics of mathematics

Prerequisite Knowledge and Skills

None

Age Appropriateness

Younger children will be able to trace the template if they have help cutting it out and if the original shape is reasonably large. Children over eight or so will be able to accomplish the activity unaided and will be able to be more creative in composing a design or image with the template.

Mathematical Idea

A tessellation is a shape that can completely cover a surface and keep on covering as big a surface as we like, repeating the shape without gaps between repetitions. For example, kitchens are often covered with square tiles, but tiles can be lots of different shapes and still completely cover the floor without gaps.

There is a legend that an ancient slave broke a tile when tiling a wall. In order to escape a beating, he created a pattern with all the tiles broken in the same way to cover the wall. Luckily, the method was acceptable to the master and became popular!

This activity explores tessellations by demonstrating that a square cut into pieces and rearranged still has the same area as the original square. Creating a tessellation shape and translating it (the mathematical word for moving it around) on the plane can result in great patterns.

Children will create new designs by rearranging parts of a square, so this activity is not only a learning opportunity but an artistic one as well. The tessellations environment is perfect for discussions of conservation of area and experimentation with translations, and it also allows for individual creativity.

HELPFUL TERMS

Area: *Area* is the number of 1 x 1 squares that it takes to cover a surface. For example, the area of a 2-inch by 3-inch rectangle is 6 square inches (that is, 2 x 3 = 6); in other words, it takes six 1-inch by 1-inch squares to cover it.

Conservation of area: This term refers to the idea that if you arrange sections of an area differently, the total area (the sum of the areas of the pieces) remains the same.

Patterns: Sets of items, such as numbers or shapes, that are continued in a predictable way are called *patterns*. Patterns created using shapes are called *geometric patterns*.

Reflection: Literally, a *reflection* is what you see when you look in a mirror, or the "mirror image" of something. In transformational geometry, reflection involves flipping an object, often to see if it looks the same (or the opposite) when flipped.

Rotation: When you move (or turn) an object in a circular path around a point called the center, you are *rotating* the object. For example, the tip of a clock hand rotates around the center of the clock; it follows a *rotational pattern*.

Square: A polygon (that is, a flat shape) with four equal sides is called a *square*.

Tessellation: A geometric pattern created by repeating a shape that can completely cover a surface forever is called a *tessellation*. A tiled floor is a simple tessellation.

A tessellation design created by rearranging the pieces of a square

Transformational geometry: The geometry of moving shapes around. For example, translations (slides), rotations (turns), and reflections (flips) are movements that are possible in *transformational geometry*.

Translation: Also known as sliding, *translation* means moving an object from one position to another in a straight-line movement.

Chapter 8

Tessellations: Making It Work

Objectives

- Children will learn about conservation of area.
- Children will enjoy visualizing and creating patterns.
- Children will experience basic transformational geometry.

Materials

- ✔ 8 ½" x 11" or 11" x 17" sheet of paper for each child
- ✔ pencil for each child
- ✔ scissors for each child
- ✔ transparent tape for each child
- ✔ small square of light cardboard for each child, about 1 ½" x 1 ½" (4 cm x 4 cm) or 2" x 2" (5 cm x 5 cm)
- ✔ crayons or colored pencils for each child or small group
- ✔ photocopy of the Tessellations Activity Sheet (on page 46) for each child

Preparation

- The well-known artist Escher made these tessellations famous. You can find lots of great pictures by searching for M. C. Escher on the web. There are also several books available that include pictures of Escher's work, such as Escher's own titles: *The Graphic Work: Introduced and Explained by the Artist,* translated by John E. Brigham (New York: Taschen, 1992), and *Escher on Escher: Exploring the Infinite,* translated by Karin Ford (New York: Abrams, 1989). Pictures of Escher tessellations are always stimulating for the kids.
- Cut out the cardboard squares according to the dimensions in the materials list. The larger size squares are easier for younger children to manipulate.

Procedure

1. Starting with a cardboard square, each child cuts out a piece of the square from the left or right side and slides that piece across the square, taping it to the opposite side (as shown in the example on the activity sheet, page 46). It may be necessary to help young children (six- or seven-year-olds) cut out the template after they draw where they want the lines cut. It is important to cut the pieces out from the side only, and not to cut past the corners.

2. Next the children cut a piece out of the bottom or top of the square, again not cutting past the corners, and tape it on the opposite side. This is a great time to discuss transformational geometry and conservation of area. You don't need to introduce the terminology to younger children, but you can still discuss the concept: Ask children if they think the new shape covers the same area as the square did.

☞ **If children are unsure if the new piece has the same area or not, it may be helpful to ask, "Where is the paper we added or removed?" to help them realize the area is the same.**

3. They then use this newly created template to trace the pattern onto a blank piece of paper. They should trace the pattern a number of times, leaving no gaps between each shape they trace, so the shapes fit together repeatedly across the page (as in the example below).

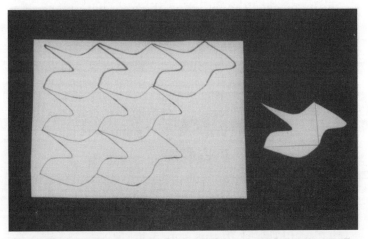

A tessellation pattern made from tracing a template repeatedly, with no gaps between shapes.

4. After they finish filling their pages with their designs, the children color them. Drawing or coloring on the finished design helps bring the shapes to life.

Suggestions

- Children translate these shapes vertically and horizontally to create the design, giving them experience with transformational geometry. This activity would usefully precede a classroom discussion of translations, if you don't discuss them during the activity.

- Teachers might want to do this one in art class to get a little extra math time!

Assessment

If the finished design could keep on going and going in all directions, in the same pattern, then the child has successfully created a tessellation pattern.

Extension Activities

- Children could create a design that forms a recognizable image, such as birds flying or fish swimming.

- Children could create different designs by starting with a rectangle or parallelogram instead of a square, or they could use equilateral triangles (arranged within hexagons so that the hexagon looks almost like a wheel with spokes) as the shape to tessellate. At first it might be easiest just to tessellate the two sides of the triangle within the hexagon (the spokes), ignoring the sides of the triangles that form the sides of the hexagon, but another challenge can be to figure out how to include the third side of each triangle when assembling the tessellated shapes.

In this activity, you get to create a work of art using just a plain old square. You could use a lot of these squares to cover a floor, just like tile in a kitchen, but other shapes will cover the same surface.

1 Starting with a cardboard square, cut out a shape from the left or right side (without cutting past the corners), slide it across the square, and tape it onto the other side. See the example below. You don't have to cut the same shape as in this example, though!

2 Cut a piece from the top or bottom, slide it to the other side, and tape it on.

3 This shape is now your template to trace onto your piece of paper. Trace the shape a number of times, so the pieces fit together on the page without any gaps. This should result in a repeated design where the pieces fit together just like a tile floor. The tessellation would keep on going forever if you had the time to trace it!

4 Now you can decorate your pattern by coloring in each section. The artist M. C. Escher was famous for pictures made in this way.

5 Do you think the area of the new pattern shape is the same as your original square? Why or why not? Can you think of any shapes, other than a square, that would work in this same way?

Start with your cardboard square . . .

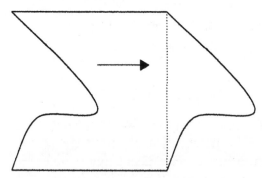

And rearrange it by cutting a piece from one side and taping that piece to the other side.

Big Ideas for Small Mathematicians, 2007 © Zephyr Press

GEOMETRIC MEMORY GAME

Activity
9

The **BIG** Idea

Our minds can picture and recall detailed geometric patterns. Sometimes kids are even better at this than grown-ups!

Content Areas in This Activity
- Geometric patterns
- Geometric recall

Process Skills Used in This Activity
- Problem solving
- Aesthetics of mathematics

Prerequisite Knowledge and Skills
None

Age Appropriateness

Children of all ages seem to enjoy playing this game. For very young children, you could reduce the number of pairs and create the disks yourself. The more difficult and subtle the patterns and the more similar the coloring of the pieces, the harder it will be to play.

Mathematical Idea

Spatial reasoning is a somewhat different skill than mathematical ability and may be improved with practice. Many children have excellent memories for pattern and shape, and this game is fun because children often legitimately beat the grown-ups at it.

Making the game pieces in a group gives experience with creating and discerning patterns, as well as creating a feeling of ownership of the game. As at least 20 pairs of the disks are needed for a good game, it works best if a reasonably large number of children are involved in the creation of the Memory pieces. Alternatively, they could be created in advance by a parent or teacher, or drawn by the grown-up and colored by children. A special theme such as fractions or rotated patterns (such as circles using rotational symmetry) might be imposed if desired. But no matter what, the patterns are bound to be interesting and worthy of discussion.

Constructing pairs of game pieces.

HELPFUL TERMS

Angle: The amount of rotation needed to get from one direction to another is an *angle*. Often we speak of the angle between two lines: This is the amount of rotation needed to get from one line to the other. It is often measured in degrees (see also *degree*).

Degree: A unit for measuring rotation, abbreviated as °, is a *degree*. A complete rotation is said to be 360 degrees. This comes from the historical thought that it took 360 days for the Earth to revolve once around the sun. Two lines at right angles form angles of ¹/₄ rotation, which is 90 degrees (that is, 360 divided by 4).

Fractions: *Fractions* are pieces into which a whole can be divided. If A has ¹/₂ of a pizza and B has ¹/₃ of the pizza, then C has the remaining ¹/₆; these three fractions make up the whole.

Hexagon: A shape with six sides is a *hexagon*. A regular hexagon is a shape with six equal sides.

Parallelogram: A four-sided shape (quadrilateral) that has parallel opposite sides is a *parallelogram*. Opposite sides are also equal. A rectangle is a special parallelogram in which the angles are 90 degrees.

Patterns: Sets of items, such as numbers or shapes, that are continued in a predictable way are called *patterns*. Patterns created using shapes are called *geometric patterns*. *Rotational patterns* are patterns created by rotating a shape or image. For example, a minute hand traces a rotational pattern around a clock face.

Pentagon: A flat geometric shape (polygon) with five sides is a *pentagon*.

Polygon: A flat (two-dimensional) shape with straight sides is a *polygon*. For example, a hexagon is a polygon with six sides.

Reflection: Literally, a *reflection* is what you see when you look in a mirror, or the "mirror image" of something. In transformational geometry, reflection involves flipping an object, often to see if it looks the same (or the opposite) when flipped.

Rotation: When you move (or turn) an object in a circular path around a point called the center, you are *rotating* the object.

Square: A polygon (that is, a flat shape) with four equal sides is called a *square*.

Symmetrical: A design with parts that are the same on both sides is a *symmetrical* design: For example, by *reflecting*, we can create a design with two identical halves.

Transformational geometry: The geometry of moving shapes around is *transformational*. For example, translations (slides), rotations (turns), and reflections (flips) are movements that are possible in *transformational geometry*.

Translation: Also known as *sliding*, *translation* means moving an object from one position to another in a straight-line movement.

Triangle: A three-sided flat (plane) figure (or polygon) is called a *triangle*.

Wedge: A pie-shaped fraction of a circle is a *wedge*.

Geometric Memory Game: Making It Work

Playing the game.

Objectives

- Children will practice shape recognition and retention.
- Children may develop an understanding of and terminology to describe patterns.

Materials

- ✔ pencil for each child
- ✔ scissors for each child or small group
- ✔ glue stick for each child or small group
- ✔ markers or colored pencils
- ✔ 20 to 40 light cardboard circles or frozen juice can lids per game set
- ✔ photocopy of the Geometric Memory Game Activity Sheet (on page 51) for each child

Preparation

- The disks can be prepared according to the directions either by the children or in advance by an adult.
- Before starting this game, have a discussion about patterns, particularly identical patterns, symmetry, shapes, and any other geometric ideas you wish to introduce, depending on the children. You might want to show example game pieces, flipping them upside down and turning them around to show the kids that the patterns may still match even if the pieces are oriented differently.

Procedure

1. Have the children create at least one pair of identical game pieces. To do this, each child first draws a pattern (using a pencil) on one of the circles on the activity sheet.

☞ **A**lternatively, you could pass out the cardboard or juice lid circles and have them draw directly on those using markers (on lids or cardboard) or colored pencils (on cardboard).

2. The second game piece will need to have exactly the same pattern as the first. The children can draw it again on the second circle on the activity sheet (or directly on the lids or cardboard), or you can photocopy their patterns to make the second piece.

3. Have the children color in both pieces, using the same colors on both so that the pieces are identical.

Coloring the pieces.

4. Then the kids cut out the circles and glue them onto the cardboard or juice lid circles. Once everyone has finished, the game is ready, unless you'd like each child to create more than one pair. Have the kids make a total of 10 to 20 pairs for each game set.

5. The game is played just like the traditional game of Memory. Shuffle the pieces and lay them face down on a table. In groups of two or three, the children take turns flipping over two game pieces. If the pieces are identical, that child keeps them and gets to take another turn. Otherwise, after everyone has a chance to see them, the child flips them back over and the next child takes a turn. The game continues until all of the pieces are gone, and the child with the most pairs wins!

Suggestions

- An adult creating the pieces might also facilitate the creation of patterns that differ more subtly, making the game more challenging.
- Another option would be for the adult to create pencil outlines of more complicated rotational designs, make a copy of each, and have each child color one pair the same.

Assessment

- Children enjoy this activity as a game, but it can be an interesting view into their ability to create, recognize, differentiate, and remember patterns and geometric images.
- Children need to notice what is the same and what is different in the pieces.

Extension Activity

Construct the game according to a particular geometric theme, such as different types of triangles or rotational symmetry, and discuss the names and classifications involved, such as different types of triangles or examples of how to rotate shapes and designs to create symmetry.

Geometric Memory Game
Activity Sheet

There are two parts to this activity: creating the game and playing it. Basically, the game is the normal memory game, where you try to pair up matching game pieces, but the shapes will be geometric patterns.

Create the Pieces

1 Using a pencil, draw a pattern or design in one of the circles below. You might try to incorporate fractions, such as a $\frac{1}{8}$ pattern that divides the circle into eight wedges, or use a pattern with some symmetry to make your design mathematically interesting.

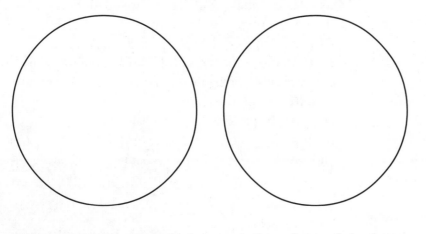

Draw a design or pattern in one circle and copy it in the second circle.

2 When you are finished with the design, trace it onto the second circle.

3 Then color in both circles exactly the same so they make an identical pair.

4 Cut out the circles and glue them onto light cardboard disks or juice container lids to make them sturdier.

5 If you are making more than one pair of disks, try to make each pair similar looking in some way to the other pairs, but not identical. This will make the game more difficult and more fun to play.

Play the Game

1 This game is played like a regular Memory game. Two to three people can play. Shuffle the disks and arrange them face down.

2 Players take turns turning over two disks, trying to get a match. Everyone gets to see the disks before the player turns them over again. If the two disks are a matching pair, the player gets to keep them and then gets another turn. Play continues until all disks are taken, and the player with the most pairs wins. Have fun practicing your geometric memory!

THE THREE BEARS

The **BIG** Idea

Our number system is based on "packages" of 10.

Content Areas in This Activity
- Addition, single digit
- Addition, double digit
- Place value to 100

Process Skills Used in This Activity
- Reasoning
- Problem solving
- Communication

Prerequisite Knowledge and Skills
- Place value to 10 (helpful)
- Addition, single digit

Age Appropriateness

The three-digit portion of this activity would be useful for children age eight or nine, when they usually start working with three-digit numbers in operations.

A simpler version of the activity could be done with younger children, starting with only two-digit addition without regrouping, working up to regrouping from the ones to the tens, and then gradually moving to include the hundreds column when appropriate.

Mathematical Idea

One of the big differences in levels of understanding of basic numeracy relates to the notion that the number system is based on place value. By this we mean that in the number 123, the 1 and the 3 mean something different. Children who have worked extensively with place value manipulatives tend to refer to the "1" as "one hundred" and the "2" as "twenty" more often than children who have just learned the rules.

Regrouping in addition and subtraction requires a good knowledge of place value to understand fully. This activity uses the analogy of receiving and shipping to model these two operations. Sometimes boxes or cases have to be packed or unpacked. In the porridge factory, the packages are the "ones," the boxes (of 10 ones) are the "tens," and the cases (of 10 boxes or 100 packages) are the "hundreds." Children model regrouping by packing or unpacking boxes and cases.

The porridge factory pieces: individual packages, boxes of 10, and cases of 100.

HELPFUL TERMS

Base: The number of symbols in a number system is its *base*. For example, in base 10 we use the symbols 0, 1, 2, 3, . . . 9, and after 9 we start again at 0 in the ones column and *regroup* the one to the next column (tens), giving 10. Base 10 came about because we have 10 fingers, so it is convenient. If we had only 6 fingers, maybe our number system would look like this: 0, 1, 2, 3, 4, 5, 10, 11, 12, 13, 14, 15, 20, 21 . . . These numbers are in base 6. The number 21 in base 6 means 2 x 6 + 1, or 13 in base 10.

Place value: *Place value* refers to the idea that a digit's column affects its value. For example, a 2 in the ones column means 2, but a 2 in the hundreds column means 200.

Regrouping: A more modern, more accurate term for carrying is *regrouping,* which means moving groups of 10 numbers from one column into the next larger column. So if a list of numbers adds up to 14 in the ones column, we write the 4 in the ones column, regroup the 10 to a 1 in the tens column, and add it there. The same applies to all columns.

Sum: *Sum* is a name for the number you get when you add two or more numbers. For example, the sum of 2 + 5 + 1 is equal to 8.

The Three Bears: Making It Work

Objectives

Children will learn the addition and subtraction methods of regrouping by using manipulatives.

Materials

- ✔ photocopy of The Three Bears Activity Sheet (on pages 57–58) for each child
- ✔ a set of base 10 blocks for each small group

— or —

- ✔ about 20 homemade "porridge" packages (small squares of paper or light cardboard), 10 to 20 small raisin boxes (which should be able to hold 10 packages each), and 5 to 9 plastic food-storage bags to be cases (which should be able to hold 10 boxes each) for each small group

The Digi-Blocks materials by Kool and Galt (available at www.louisekool.com) are base 10 blocks that actually resemble boxes, ideal for this activity.

Preparation

If you don't use base 10 blocks, you will need to prepare the porridge pieces in advance by cutting out of paper or light cardboard the package squares, in addition to gathering enough raisin boxes and plastic food-storage bags.

Procedure 1: Addition

1. Have the children get into groups of three and decide who will be Baby Bear, who will be Mother Bear, and who will be Father Bear. It would be ideal if one of the group members could be an older helper.

2. Explain that the Bear family works in a porridge factory, and that each bear has a different storage area in the factory. Baby Bear's storage area can hold only 9 packages of porridge. Show the children what the packages look like—the individual squares—and hand out 20 packages to the Baby Bear in each group for use later.

3. Explain next that Mother Bear's storage area is a bit larger and can hold up to 9 boxes of porridge. Show the children what a box looks like—a strip of 10 squares or a raisin box—and hand out 10 to 20 boxes to the Mother Bear in each group.

4. Finally, explain that Father Bear has the largest storage area of all. He can hold up to 9 cases. Show the children what a case looks like—a sheet of 10 strips, or 100 squares, or a plastic food-storage bag—and hand out 5 to 9 cases to the Father Bear in each group.

5. Walk the children through the first or all of the following addition and subtraction problems. Start with a simple addition problem using just packages and boxes. Remind them that each of them can hold only 9 of their items. If they have 10 at any point, they must group those 10 and give them to the next person: Baby Bear gives groups of 10 packages to Mother Bear to box, and Mother Bear gives groups of 10 boxes to Father Bear.

6. Tell the children that Baby Bear has 6 packages. Have each Baby Bear count out 6 squares, pushing the others aside.

7. Mother Bear has 4 boxes. Have each Mother Bear count out 4 boxes and push the others aside.

8. Next, tell them that 7 new packages have arrived. Have Baby Bear group 10 packages and give them to Mother Bear. Baby Bear could hand Mother Bear the 10 packages, and she could put them in a small raisin box or trade them for a strip of 10 squares.

9. Mother Bear now has another box. Ask the children how many packages Baby Bear now has (3), and how many boxes Mother Bear now has (5). Show the children on the activity sheet (or write on the board) the problem they just figured out:

$$
\begin{array}{r}
46 \\
+\ 7 \\
\hline
53
\end{array}
$$

10. Next the children try a problem with packages, boxes, *and* cases. (Alternatively, you could make up additional problems using just packages and boxes if the children need more practice.) Start by telling them that they just received another shipment of 1 case, 6 boxes, and 8 packages.

11. Have the children count out each of these to add to his or her current stock. Baby Bear already had 3 packages, so receiving 8 more should give him or her a total of 11. Baby Bear should then group 10 of these packages as a box to give to Mother Bear, keeping 1 package.

12. Mother Bear had 5 boxes, so 6 boxes from the shipment and 1 box from Baby Bear give her 12

boxes in all. Now Mother Bear must group 10 of her boxes into a case to give to Father Bear, keeping 2 boxes.

13. Father Bear received 1 case from the shipment and 1 case from Mother Bear, so he now has 2 cases.

> ☞ **A**lternating this activity with more traditional addition and subtraction questions may be helpful.

14. Show the children on the activity sheet, or write on the board, the problem they just solved.

$$\begin{array}{r} 168 \\ + \ 53 \\ \hline 221 \end{array}$$

221 means

2 hundreds (or cases)

2 tens (or boxes)

1 one (or package)

15. Continue with addition problems using the amounts in the chart on page 58 or making up your own amounts for the children to try.

Procedure 2: Subtraction

1. Now it's time to see what happens when the Bear family starts selling porridge! Tell the children that when they receive orders for porridge, they will need to take those orders away from what they have. If a customer wants more boxes than Mother Bear has on hand, then Father Bear can unpack a case to give Mother Bear more boxes. If a customer wants more packages than Baby Bear has on hand, then Mother Bear can unpack a box to give Baby Bear more packages.

2. Start with the following example: Father Bear has 2 cases, Mother Bear has 5 boxes, and Baby Bear has 6 packages. Wait for all groups of children to gather the correct number in front of them.

3. Now tell them a customer wants 7 boxes. Mother Bear has only 5 boxes, so Father Bear will have to unpack one of his cases to give Mother Bear 10 boxes to add to her 5 so she can give the customer 7. (You or another child in the class can pretend to be the customer, or the children could just push the materials aside into a "customer area.")

4. Now ask the children how many cases, boxes, and packages each has. Father Bear should have 1 case left. Mother Bear should have 8 boxes left. Baby Bear still has 6 packages. Show them on the activity sheet, or write on the board, the subtraction problem they just solved.

$$\begin{array}{r} 256 \\ - \ 70 \\ \hline 186 \end{array}$$

5. Have the children try more subtraction problems, such as the ones in the chart on page 58, or make up your own. Ultimately, children can progress to working out these problems on their own.

Suggestions

- Children who have memorized the addition and subtraction regrouping rules without understanding will be totally lost in the activity. If this is the case, keep the activity to just ones and tens (packages and boxes) for a while.

- This activity is particularly important for children having trouble understanding the traditional addition and subtraction procedures of regrouping. In this activity, the regrouping operation is modeled by packing and unpacking boxes and cases. Children with a poor grasp of place value may need support in this activity until they get the idea.

Assessment

- Assessment is likely to be ongoing, coupled with traditional addition and subtraction questions.

- If children can model an addition or subtraction question with regrouping using manipulatives such as these, then they have a thorough understanding of place value.

Extension Activity

Have the children try a sequence of products being received and products being ordered. Can they make the stock and the accounting system balance?

This game works well for three people to play together. Each person is one of the three bears. Baby Bear has only a small storage area and can't store more than 9 packages of porridge at a time. Mother Bear has a little more room—she can handle up to 9 boxes. Each box contains 10 packages. And Father Bear handles the cases—up to 9 cases at a time. Each case contains 10 boxes.

Receiving New Stock

1 When new product arrives from the other side of the factory to be packaged, the bears (that's you!) try to box and case as much as possible. If stock is already on hand, some existing stock may need re-arranging. For example, if Mother Bear has 4 boxes, and Baby Bear has 6 packages, and you receive 7 more packages, you'll have 4 boxes and 13 packages.

2 Baby Bear sends 10 packages to be boxed. This box of 10 packages is added to Mother Bear's stock. Baby Bear keeps the rest. So Baby Bear now has 3 packages, and Mother Bear now has 5 boxes. This is like

original amount: 46

new amount: 7

new total: 53

At the moment, Mother Bear has 5 boxes, and Baby Bear has 3 packages.

MODELING THE FIRST EXAMPLE

Materials on hand:

Baby Bear's 6 packages

Mother Bear's 4 boxes

Now they get a new shipment:

New shipment of 7 packages

So Baby Bear must box up the packages:

New shipment of 7 packages

The 3 packages Baby Bear has left

+

Use 4 of the new shipment with the 6 Baby Bear already had on hand to make a new box of 10 to give to Mother Bear.

The result:

Mother Bear now has 5 boxes, and Baby Bear has 3 packages—53 packages total!

3 Let's say we now receive a shipment of 1 case, 6 boxes, and 8 packages. Baby Bear already has 3 packages and gets 8 more, which is 11 in all. So Baby Bear sends 10 to be boxed by Mother Bear and keeps the last package.

4 Mother Bear has 5 boxes on hand, plus the 6 new boxes, and 1 new one from Baby Bear. This makes 12 in all. So she sends 10 to be put in a case by Father Bear and keeps the other 2.

5 So Father Bear has the 1 newly arrived case and the 1 from Mother Bear, or 2 in all. We call this number

221
and it means
2 hundreds (or cases)
2 tens (or boxes)
1 one (or single package)

6 Try some different initial amounts by giving each player some pieces and then processing a newly received amount. You can make up your own or try the ones below. In each case, work through the situation as above, and conclude with the total stock now on hand.

	Cases	Boxes	Packages	Total
1. On hand	0	7	3	_____
Received	1	5	0	_____
2. On hand	2	9	6	_____
Received	1	0	4	_____
3. On hand	2	3	9	_____
Received	2	6	23	_____
4. On hand	1	6	4	_____
Received	0	12	16	_____

Porridge Sales

1 In the middle of all this activity, sometimes you get orders for porridge. If customers want more boxes than you have on hand but you do have cases, you can unpack a case and use the 10 boxes. This is subtraction.

2 For example, you have on hand 2 cases, 5 boxes, and 6 packages, and a customer wants 7 boxes. So Father Bear unpacks 1 case and you get 1 case, 15 boxes, and 6 packages *less* 7 boxes for the customer.

3 What do you have after sending out the 7 boxes? 1 case, 8 boxes, and 6 packages.

$$\begin{array}{r} 256 \\ -\ 70 \\ \hline 186 \end{array}$$

4 Now let's say more customers want to order porridge. Try the subtraction problems using the numbers below, or make up your own.

	Cases	Boxes	Packages	Total
1. On hand	2	4	6	_____
Ordered	1	2	3	_____
2. On hand	3	2	5	_____
Ordered	1	3	0	_____
3. On hand	2	3	4	_____
Ordered	0	5	6	_____
4. On hand	3	6	5	_____
Ordered	2	6	6	_____

Big Ideas for Small Mathematicians, 2007 © Zephyr Press

PARTY FRACTIONS

Activity 11

The **BIG** Idea

Equivalent fractions are found in lots of food servings, and we all like to get our fair share!

Content Areas in This Activity
- Equivalent fractions
- Equivalent measures

Process Skills Used in This Activity
Reasoning

Prerequisite Knowledge and Skills
Fraction notation and meaning

Age Appropriateness

The first game would be more appropriate for primary children (ages six to eight). Either game is appropriate for ages nine and ten. Made-up games can work with any age.

Mathematical Idea

Fractions are often one of the first mathematical topics with which children have insufficient concrete experience to understand fully and soon resort to memorization—the first step toward developing mathphobia later on. Game environments and those related to food are great spaces for experiencing and playing with concrete fractional materials. This activity is only one possible example. Cutting fruits at snack time provides good experience too. For example, if one child gets a half of an apple, and another gets two quarter sections, we can ask, "Who got more?"

If you need to resort to algebraic methods to be sure of a correct answer quickly, recall that $^2/_4 = ^1/_2$ (2 divides into both 2 and 4 to give $^1/_2$). The idea behind this is that dividing everything by 2 is like pairing the fractional pieces; that is, the 2 out of 4 (the $^2/_4$) is like 1 out of 2 of the paired pieces. We used to say "cancel the 2" but now the phrase "divides into" is used more in school because it is more accurate. These algebraic skills are not needed for this activity, and in fact it is better to work with the concrete materials long before introducing the technical skills.

The notion of equivalence may not be immediately obvious to a child, and he or she may not agree initially that two quarters and one half are the same. It is the discussion and the construction of these notions for the individual child that is most important at this stage.

HELPFUL TERMS

Diameter: The distance across a circle, through the center, is called the *diameter*.

Fractions: *Fractions* are pieces into which a whole can be divided. If A has ¹/₂ of a pizza and B has ¹/₃ of the pizza, then C has the remaining ¹/₆; these three fractions make up the whole.

Rotation: When you move (or turn) an object in a circular path around a point called the center, you are *rotating* the object. For example, the tip of a clock hand rotates around the center of the clock; it follows a rotational pattern.

Wedge: A pie-shaped fraction of a circle is called a *wedge*.

A birthday cake with eight pieces (eighths).

Party Fractions: Making It Work

Objectives

Children will gain an understanding of fractions, particularly equivalent fractions, geometrically.

Materials

- ✔ ten cardboard circles at least 8" (20 cm) in diameter for each group of four children
- ✔ a blank sheet of paper with an 8" (20-cm) circular outline drawn on it for each child
- ✔ a die for each group of four children
- ✔ markers for each group of four children
- ✔ photocopy of the Party Fractions Activity Sheet (on pages 63–64) for each child
- ✔ scissors

Preparation

- Prepare the circles by cutting them to size. Make sure all circles are identical in size. You can also use paper instead of cardboard, as shown in the photos, but cardboard will produce a sturdier product. The sheet of paper with the circle drawn on it will be the cake (or pizza) pan and should not be colored in.

- If you wish, you can decorate and cut out the cake pieces in advance, following the directions opposite, or just draw on the fractions (with at least two of each circle divided into halves, thirds, quarters, sixths, and eighths), leaving the decoration for the children as part of the fun. (One circle for each set of fractions is enough for just two children playing.)

A more professional product could be obtained by color copying a large photograph of a cake or pizza from an ad or a package label, writing the fractions on in black marker, laminating, and cutting up as necessary.

Another twist: Let each child decorate a pizza or cake as he or she chooses, then laminate the circle and cut out the fractional pieces.

Procedure 1: Filling the Cake

1. First, have the kids get into groups of four. Give each group ten circles to decorate as cakes (or pizzas), using the markers. An older helper might be useful in each group for six- or seven-year-olds. (If you use smaller groups, such as two or three, fewer circles will suffice.)

2. Help each group of four divide the ten circles into fractional wedges. Two of the circles should be divided into halves, two into thirds, two into quarters, two into eighths, and two into sixths. You can have them draw lines to divide the circles and then cut them out, or you can draw the lines for them to cut along. The blank circular outline will be the pan to fill. Depending on the age and understanding of the children, this is a good time to discuss the idea of fractions as parts of a whole as well as to review fractional notation, pointing out that $1/2$ means they

have one piece of a cake (or pizza) cut into two equal pieces, $1/4$ means one piece of a cake cut into four equal pieces, and so on.

3. To play the first game, each child in the group gets an empty pan (paper circle). All of the fractional wedges go into a draw pile.

4. The children take turns rolling the die and taking or returning the fractional wedge that the die indicates, as shown in the box on the activity sheet (page 63). Each child tries to fill his or her cake exactly using the wedges, with no wedges left over.

The idea of the activity is to get children thinking and talking about equivalent fractions: what pieces are the same. If they have trouble seeing if the pieces they have make a whole or not, it might be helpful to group pieces together. For example, two one-quarter pieces should be put side by side to help them see that this is half the pizza, or two sixths put next to a third with the question "Do you think these two sixths are the same as the one third?" and then "How much of the cake do all of these cover so far?"

The use of equivalent fractions in mathematics is meant to provide the most useful and simple representation of a particular fraction for a particular context. This game provides a context for such discussions. However, if the discussion evolves into a related discussion or investigation as play progresses, continue in the new direction rather than forcing a particular game to be played.

Procedure 2: Servings

1. For the second game, each child starts with a combination of pieces that make a whole cake (a full pan). The kids can continue from the previous game, after everyone has filled his or her cake pan, or they can take turns drawing wedges until each has a full cake before starting the second game. Pull all half wedges out of the game completely.

2. Have one player in each group roll one die to determine whether the goal of the game will be to split the cakes into three servings or four servings. A roll of 3 or less is 3 servings; a roll of 4 or more is 4. The object of the game will be for the children to split their cakes in some way to serve three people or four people equally.

3. The children take turns rolling the die. They then exchange one wedge of their own for a wedge from the draw pile that matches the roll of the die. The rolls are worth the same as in the box on page 63, except a roll of 2 is also a wild card roll, instead of representing a half piece. A player can also choose to refuse a roll. The wild card rolls (1 or 2) mean the player can pick up *or* return a piece of his or her choice with no trade.

4. Play continues until one person splits his or her cake into the servings specified. For example, if the goal is to serve four people, three one-quarter wedges and two one-eighths would work.

Filling up the cake!

Suggestions

- For those children just beginning to learn fractional notation, you or the children could write on each piece with black marker the fraction each piece represents.

- Children often spontaneously invent games of their own. Encourage them!

Assessment

Informally observe whether the children play the game successfully.

Extension Activity

Add a new cake cut up into 12 pieces to the choices. Use a roll of 1 to represent one of these new pieces, called *twelfths*. This will make both games harder!

11a Party Fractions Activity Sheet

This activity includes two different games for you and your friends to play. With the help of an adult, you create cakes (or pizzas) with pieces of all different sizes. Can you put the cake back together using the pieces?

Filling the Cake

1 First get into a group with three other people. As a group, you will decorate ten circles to look like birthday cakes (or pizzas), using markers.

2 On your own or with help, divide the cakes into pieces (called *wedges*) of different sizes by drawing lines from the center.

- Divide two cakes each into two equal wedges, or *halves*.

- Divide two cakes each into three equal wedges, or *thirds*.

- Divide two cakes each into four equal wedges, or *quarters*.

- Divide two cakes each into six equal wedges, or *sixths*.

- Divide the last cakes into eight equal wedges, or *eighths*.

> Folding the paper is a simple way to create the lines that are straight and divide the cake equally.

3 After dividing the cakes, cut out all of the wedges and put them into a draw pile. Each of you then takes a cake pan (a blank circle), and you're ready to start the first game.

4 To play the first game, you take turns rolling the die. Each number on the die represents a wedge from the draw pile, as shown below. Take the wedge from the draw pile that matches your roll and place it on your cake pan. The goal is to fill up your cake pan exactly. If you roll a 1, you can take any wedge *or* return one of your wedges, but you can't trade your wedge with one in the pile.

Roll of 1: wild card—choose any wedge or return a wedge of your choice to the pile

Roll of 2: a half

Roll of 3: a third

Roll of 4: a quarter

Roll of 5: an eighth

Roll of 6: a sixth

Servings

1 For the second game, you start with a combination of wedges that makes a full cake. If you play this right after the first game, after everyone has completly covered a whole cake pan, you will each have a full cake to start. Otherwise, everyone can take turns choosing one wedge at a time until everyone's cake is full. Set the half pieces aside. You won't need them for this game.

2 One player now rolls the die once to determine how many people each of you needs to serve with your cake, either three or four people. A roll of 3 or less is 3 servings; a roll of 4 or more is 4. If the player rolls a 4 or more, for example, then everyone's goal is to divide his or her cake in a way that will serve four people equally.

3 After rolling to decide the goal for your group, take turns rolling the die and trading a particular wedge on your cake for the one in the center pile that matches your roll. You may also choose to refuse a roll completely. Note: For this game, because you aren't using the half wedges, a roll of 1 or 2 is a wild card roll. If you roll a wild card (a roll of 1 or 2) then you can pick up any wedge or return any wedge, but you can't trade. The winner is the first person who can split his or her cake into the servings specified the fastest. For example, to serve four people, three one-quarter wedges and two one-eighths would work.

4 Enjoy making up your own fraction games, too! Add more wedges to the game as needed.

You don't have to serve four people with four wedges. You can give one person two (or more) wedges that equal one large wedge. If you give three people each a quarter of your cake, then what two wedges could you give to the fourth person? In other words, if you filled up three quarters of your cake, what two wedges could you use to fill up that last quarter?

Big Ideas for Small Mathematicians, 2007 © Zephyr Press

SUNCATCHER REFLECTIONS

Activity

12

The **BIG** Idea

Reflections and rotations make great patterns—and there's even a connection to fractions and measuring angles.

Content Areas in This Activity

- Division as partitioning
- Division, single-digit divisor (optional)
- Division with calculator (optional)
- Angle measurement
- Circle measurement
- Geometric patterning
- Transformational geometry (including rotational symmetry)

Process Skills Used in This Activity

- Hypothesizing
- Creativity
- Aesthetics of mathematics

Prerequisite Knowledge and Skills

Division, single digit (helpful)

Age Appropriateness

If you precut the circles and wedges, young children will be able to create the designs. Adjust the discussion of mathematics to the age and understanding of the children.

For example, you could limit your discussion to just the idea of a reflection (flip) and omit discussion of measurement for six- and seven-year-olds. All children will be able to enjoy the creation of beautiful symmetrical patterns.

Mathematical Idea

Mathematical ideas are sometimes studied in isolation, but often the connections between areas, such as measurement, geometry, patterning, and algebra, are most interesting and important. In this activity, children explore the mathematical basis of a kaleidoscope, making acetate suncatchers in the process.

First they will use mirrors to explore rotational patterns. The key idea to discover is that when the mirrors are held at an angle that divides exactly into 360 degrees an even number of times, the pie-shaped pattern will reflect in each mirror and make an exact and complete rotational pattern. For example, 360° ÷ 6 pieces = 60° and 6 is an even number of pattern pieces. Six pieces of 60 degrees each will exactly rotate around the circle. If the number of pieces is not even (divisible by two), the pattern cannot alternate (reflect) with each rotation. Other angles that divide into 360 degrees are 90 degrees and 45 degrees. If you hold two mirrors at any of these angles on top of a pattern, the pattern will repeat itself in the mirrors in a full circle. Try it!

HELPFUL TERMS

Angle: The amount of rotation needed to get from one direction to another is an *angle*. Often we speak of the angle between two lines: This is the amount of rotation needed to get from one line to the other. It is often measured in degrees (see also *degree*).

Degree: A unit for measuring rotation, abbreviated as °, is a *degree*. A complete rotation is said to be 360 degrees. This comes from the historical thought that it took 360 days for the Earth to revolve once around the sun. Two lines at right angles form angles of ¼ rotation, which is 90 degrees (that is, 360 divided by 4).

Divisibility: The *divisibility* of a number describes whether any numbers can be divided into it with no remainder. For example, 10, 15, and 20 are divisible by 5. The divisibility rule for 5 is that 5 will divide evenly (with no remainder) into numbers that end in 5 or 0.

Factors: Numbers that divide evenly (with no remainder) into a number are *factors* of that number (see also *divisibility*).

Fractions: *Fractions* are pieces into which a whole can be divided. If A has ½ of a pizza and B has ⅓ of the pizza, then C has the remaining ⅙; these three fractions make up the whole.

Measurement: A way of counting or quantifying distance or area, using a particular unit, is *measurement*. In this activity, children may use a protractor to measure degrees in an angle.

Patterns: Sets of items, such as numbers or shapes, that are continued in a predictable way are called *patterns*. Patterns created using shapes are called *geometric patterns*. *Linear patterns* change by the same amount each time: for example, 2, 4, 6, 8, . . . (changing by 2) or red, blue, red, blue. *Nonlinear patterns* change by a different amount each time: for example, 2, 4, 7, 11, 16, . . . (changing by 2, then 3, then 4, then 5, and so on) or red, blue, red, blue, blue, red, blue, blue, blue, . . . *Rotational patterns* are patterns created by rotating a shape or image. For example, a minute hand traces a rotational pattern around a clock face.

Reflection: Literally, a *reflection* is what you see when you look in a mirror, or the "mirror image" of something. In transformational geometry, reflection involves flipping an object, often to see if it looks the same (or the opposite) when flipped.

Rotation: When you move (or turn) an object in a circular path around a point called the center, you are *rotating* the object.

Rotational symmetry: *Rotational symmetry* describes a design that repeats itself as we trace out the rotation and is the same every fixed amount.

Symmetrical: A design with parts that are the same on both sides is a *symmetrical* design: For example, by reflecting, we can create a design with two reflected halves.

Transformational geometry: The geometry of moving shapes around is *transformational*. For example, translations (slides), rotations (turns), and reflections (flips) are movements that are possible in *transformational geometry*.

Translation: Also known as sliding, *translation* means moving an object from one position to another in a straight-line movement.

Wedge: A pie-shaped fraction of a circle is called a *wedge*.

Some commercial kaleidoscopes have ten pieces around each rotation, an angle of 360 degrees divided by 10 degrees, or 36 degrees, but this requires too much measuring precision for this activity.

This activity involves concepts such as division, measurement of angles, fractions, reflections, rotations, rotational symmetry, and patterning—all of the ideas reinforce one another.

Seeing rotated patterns in a pair of mirrors.

Suncatcher Reflections: Making It Work

Objectives

- Children will investigate the mathematical ideas that make kaleidoscopes work.
- Children will create interesting rotational patterns with reflections.
- Children will connect ideas of angle measurement, fractions, and division (optional).

Materials

- ✔ two small rectangular mirrors for each child
- ✔ scissors for each child
- ✔ color magazine or book picture for each child
- ✔ 8 ½" x 11" sheet of clear acetate transparency or tracing paper for each child
- ✔ water-soluble transparency pens or colored pencils (if using tracing paper)
- ✔ 8 ½" x 11" black construction paper for each frame
- ✔ glue for each child or small group
- ✔ hole punch
- ✔ suction cup and string for each suncatcher
- ✔ photocopy of the Suncatcher Reflections Activity Sheet (on pages 71–72) for each child

Preparation

- Using the templates on page 68, cut the circle and three sizes of wedges out of the acetate or tracing paper for each child. The acetate is easier to use and produces a nicer final product than the tracing paper, although both will work for this activity.

- If you plan to mount the finished designs, cut a frame out of black construction paper to fit the size of each circle for each child. The hole in the frame needs to be slightly smaller than the circle so the frame will overlap.

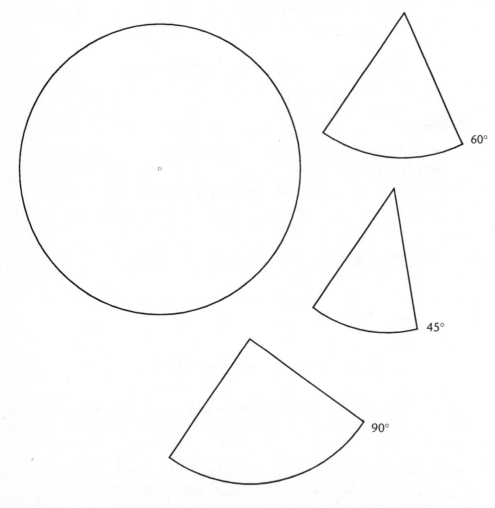

Templates for acetate circle and wedges (enlarge as desired).

Procedure

1. Have the children spend some time investigating angles with pairs of mirrors on top of a color picture. Young children will enjoy just looking at the different images that appear in the mirrors as they change the angles. With older children, this is an opportunity to discuss the basics of angles and transformational geometry, such as degrees, rotation, rotational symmetry, rotational patterns, and reflection. The children must hold the mirrors upright, touching on one edge, rotating one mirror to change the angle between them.

2. Discuss the fact that certain angles produce clear images in the mirrors, but as they rotate the mirrors away from these angles, they get a blur in the back of the pattern. With older children, you can discuss which angles produce a clear image (those that divide into 360 with an even result) and those that don't. With younger children, just have fun looking at the different angles.

3. Pass out the circles and wedges and explain that the wedges have angles that will work to create a rotational pattern. That is, the wedge angles match some of the mirror angles that worked to get a clear image. You might show them with four 90-degree wedges how four of them fit exactly on the circle, then repeat this with six 60-degree wedges and eight 45-degree wedges.

4. Next explain to the children that they are going to create a suncatcher using the circles and a wedge. Have them choose the wedge they wish to use and place it anywhere on their color pictures. The smaller-angled wedges will make more complicated designs.

Examining a commercial kaleidoscope or two can be an interesting way to enhance the investigation of angles, wedges, and rotational patterns.

5. Using the transparency pens (with acetate) or the colored pencils (with tracing paper), each child traces a portion of a picture onto the wedge, making sure to go all the way to edges of the wedge. This wedge will be the pattern piece. Emphasize that they are not trying to trace a complete picture inside the wedge. That's why tracing the pattern is better than drawing on the wedge freehand. Freehand drawings, such as a heart or flower in the center, are often symmetrical and do not go to the edge, which makes tracing the wedge image repeatedly on the circle much harder to do. The idea of a reflected image also gets lost because a symmetrical image looks the same reflected.

Tracing the pattern wedge.

6. After they have all finished tracing onto their pattern pieces, have the children place their mirrors along each straight edge of their pattern pieces. The pattern each child sees in the mirrors is what he or she will end up tracing onto the circle.

7. Have the children begin by placing the circle on the pattern piece so that the rounded edges line up and the tip of the wedge is in the center of the circle, then trace the design onto the circle.

8. Next the children will reflect the pattern piece (flip it over), and place it under the circle so that one edge lines up with the edge of what they just traced (that is, so that the wedge designs are right next to each other without overlapping).

A key point in the creation of the suncatcher is to reflect the pattern after each tracing. Remind children that this is what the mirror does. They can check their emerging designs with the mirrors held over the initial wedge every so often to ensure that what they are creating is the same pattern they see in the mirrors.

9. They continue tracing their design, flipping the pattern piece each time, until they've completed the circle. The pieces should fill the space reasonably well.

10. After completing their designs, the children color them in. If you wish, you can provide a black frame and help them, if necessary, to glue around the edge of the suncatcher and attach it to the frame.

11. Help them punch a hole in each suncatcher or frame, loop the string through and tie it, then wrap it around the suction cup (or around the hook on the suction cup, if it has one). Now the suncatchers are ready to hang on any window!

Suggestions

This activity can be a pleasing exercise in creating an interesting kaleidoscopelike pattern, or it can be a more detailed lesson in any or all of the following mathematical concepts: angle measurement, division, fractions, and transformational geometry. All of these ideas and their interconnections are present in the activity, and it is up to you how much discussion of these topics is desirable. I have used this activity embedded in a fourth-grade lesson on transformational geometry and made connections to division and angular measurement. I have used it with both younger and older children as a pleasurable introduction to the mathematics (not necessarily the terminology) governing kaleidoscopes, which is the topic of the next activity (page 73). Encourage the children to enjoy the patterns, to notice and discuss the mathematics, and to discover their beauty, all as appropriate to the interests of the children.

Assessment

- The finished suncatcher should show an understanding of the role of the mirror (that is, the children flip the wedge as they trace to mimic the action of the mirror).

- If you discuss deeper mathematical ideas in conjunction with this activity, such as the idea that six pieces in a pattern must mean each piece has a 60-degree angle because 360 divided by 6 is 60, then you can determine understanding by asking children to explain these concepts.

Extension Activity

Have the kids cut out their own circles and wedges, using a protractor to measure the angles and experimenting with which wedges will work and why. They could also work on a design with a smaller wedge angle, such as 36 degrees, but that will require patience and precision.

Suncatcher Reflections Activity Sheet

In this activity, you get to create a suncatcher based on the reflections you see in a mirror!

1 Using two small mirrors, hold them together in a wedge shape over a color picture. Look into the mirrors and explore what happens as you change the angle between them.

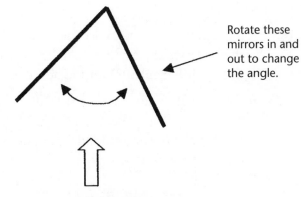

Rotate these mirrors in and out to change the angle.

Look in here.

A top-down view of how to hold the mirrors together at an angle on top of your picture.

2 At certain angles, you will see a clear set of images. For example, at 90 degrees you should see four images reflected in the mirrors as you look into them. (Ask an adult for help if you're not sure which angle is a 90-degree angle, or hold your two mirrors along the corner of a book.) Some angles work to give a clear pattern, and as you rotate away from these angles you will get a blur in the back of the pattern. Try it! Discuss with others how to find the angles that work.

3 In this activity you will make a suncatcher based on one of the angles that makes a complete rotational pattern. These are the angles that created a clear image, without any blurring, when you looked into the mirrors.

> A *rotational pattern* is a pattern you create by rotating something, such as a shape, around in a circle. For example, a minute hand traces a rotational pattern around a clock face.

4 Choose a wedge to be your pattern piece.

Suncatcher Reflections
Activity Sheet

5 Place the wedge on a color picture. Using a colored pencil (if the wedge is made of tracing paper) or a transparency pen (if the wedge is made out of transparency paper), trace a part of the outline of the picture onto the wedge pattern piece. It is important that you trace something rather than draw it, so the design goes right to the edges of the wedge. For example, you might have something like this:

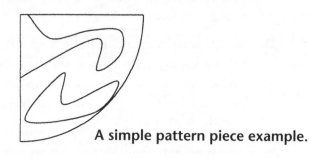

A simple pattern piece example.

6 Hold the mirrors on the straight edges of the wedge pattern piece and look in. The pattern you see is what you are going to create on your large circle. The large circle will become your finished suncatcher.

7 First place the circle on the pattern piece and trace the pattern piece design on the circle as is, being careful to line up the center and the rounded edges.

8 Now, what do you have to do before you can trace the next section of the rotated pattern? Remember what the mirror does! It reflects, so you want to reflect the pattern piece (flip it over) before lining it up with what you just traced and tracing again. Hold a mirror on the edge of the wedge to check your design.

9 Continue tracing all around until the design is complete.

10 You can now color your suncatcher brightly. Color each part to make a symmetrical design (a design with identical elements) for the best effect.

11 You can mount your suncatcher by gluing it on a black construction-paper frame. Punch a hole for string, wrap the string around a suction cup, and hang it in the window.

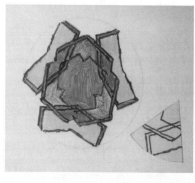

A finished suncatcher and the pattern piece used to create it.

Big Ideas for Small Mathematicians, 2007 © Zephyr Press

KALEIDOSCOPE

The **BIG** Idea

Lots of great toys use mathematics, such as the kaleidoscope. You can build your own!

Content Areas in This Activity

- Angle measurement (optional)
- Circle measurement (optional)
- Geometric patterning
- Transformational geometry (optional)

Process Skills Used in This Activity

- Creativity
- Aesthetics of mathematics

Prerequisite Knowledge and Skills

Activity 12 (helpful)

Age Appropriateness

All children will be able to create the kaleidoscope but will need the holes prepunched into the can as well as either the tubes cut shorter for the purse mirrors or the custom mirrors available and ready to use.

Mathematical Idea

This activity can be done after the previous one (on page 65) or on its own. The kaleidoscope itself was invented by an Englishman named David Brewster early in the twentieth century and has remained popular ever since. The mathematics behind the kaleidoscope are examined in the previous activity, Suncatcher Reflections.

After doing the previous activity, it's easier to actually calculate the angle of the mirrors when we look into commercial kaleidoscopes. All we have to do is count the number of images we see going around the circle in each section. For example, if we see eighths in the design, we know the mirror angle is 360 ÷ 8 or 45 degrees. Sixty degrees is a popular angle for kaleidoscopes, and it is the one we will use here. If we create an equilateral triangle out of three mirrors placed as a triangular prism with the mirrors facing in, we know the angles between the mirrors are 60 degrees because equilateral triangles have 60-degree angles. It is this construction of mirrors that makes the kaleidoscope work.

Constructing a homemade kaleidoscope is easy!

HELPFUL TERMS

Angle: The amount of rotation needed to get from one direction to another is an *angle*. Often we speak of the angle between two lines: This is the amount of rotation needed to get from one line to the other. It is often measured in degrees (see also *degree*).

Degree: A unit for measuring rotation, abbreviated as °, is a *degree*. A complete rotation is said to be 360 degrees. This comes from the historical thought that it took 360 days for the Earth to revolve once around the sun. Two lines at right angles form angles of ¼ rotation, which is 90 degrees (that is, 360 divided by 4).

Divisibility: The *divisibility* of a number describes whether any numbers can be divided into it with no remainder. For example, 10, 15, and 20 are divisible by 5. The *divisibility rule* for 5 is that 5 will divide evenly (with no remainder) into numbers that end in 5 or 0.

Factors: Numbers that divide evenly (with no remainder) into a number are *factors* of that number (see also *divisibility*).

Fractions: *Fractions* are pieces into which a whole can be divided. If A has ½ of a pizza and B has ⅓ of the pizza, then C has the remaining ⅙; these three fractions make up the whole.

Measurement: A way of counting or quantifying distance or area, using a particular unit, is *measurement*. In this activity, children may use a protractor to measure degrees in an angle.

Patterns: Sets of items, such as numbers or shapes, that are continued in a predictable way are called *patterns*. Patterns created using shapes are called *geometric patterns*. *Linear patterns* change by the same amount each time: for example, 2, 4, 6, 8, . . . (changing by 2) or red, blue, red, blue. *Nonlinear patterns* change by a different amount each time: for example, 2, 4, 7, 11, 16, . . . (changing by 2, then 3, then 4, then 5, and so on) or red, blue, red, blue, blue, red, blue, blue, blue, . . . *Rotational patterns* are patterns created by rotating a shape or image. For example, a minute hand traces a rotational pattern around a clock face.

Reflection: Literally, a *reflection* is what you see when you look in a mirror, or the "mirror image" of something. In transformational geometry, reflection involves flipping an object, often to see if it looks the same (or the opposite) when flipped.

Rotation: When you move (or turn) an object in a circular path around a point called the center, you are *rotating* the object.

Rotational symmetry: *Rotational symmetry* describes a design that repeats itself as we trace out the rotation and is the same every fixed amount.

Symmetrical: A design with parts that are the same on both sides is a *symmetrical* design: For example, by reflecting, we can create a design with two identical halves.

Transformational geometry: The geometry of moving shapes around is *transformational*. For example, translations (slides), rotations (turns), and reflections (flips) are movements that are possible in *transformational geometry*.

Translation: Also known as sliding, *translation* means moving an object from one position to another in a straight-line movement.

Kaleidoscope: Making It Work

Objectives

- Children will create a mathematical object using the mathematical ideas from activity 12 (on page 65).
- Children will enjoy understanding and creating a mathematical toy.

Materials

✔ potato chip can with clear lid, 9" (23 cm) tall, for each child

✔ hammer

✔ nail (reasonably large)

✔ about ¼ cup clear beads for each child

✔ 4" x 4" (10 cm x 10 cm) piece of acetate transparency or other transparent plastic for each child

✔ water-soluble transparency pen for each child

✔ transparent tape

✔ masking tape

✔ scissors for each child

✔ three rectangular purse mirrors or custom-cut mirrored glass to fit in can for each child (see Preparation for more information on custom-cut glass)

✔ half-sheet of tissue for each child

✔ photocopy of Kaleidoscope Activity Sheet (on page 78) for each child

No two kaleidoscopes are ever alike! Be sure to look at everyone's.

Preparation

- Punch a hole, ⅛ inch to ¼ inch (3 mm to 6 mm), in the center of the metal end of each chip can with a hammer and nail. This will be the hole the children will look through into the kaleidoscope.
- The directions that follow and on the activity sheet have the children cutting their own acetate circles, but you can precut these for younger children, following the directions.
- If you use purse mirrors, you will need to cut off the can at the open end to just over ½ inch (1.5 cm) longer than the mirrors lengthwise inside the can.
- If you decide to use custom-cut glass (which will give you a superior product), you will need to have each set of three pieces cut at a glass store. The size is about 2 ⅖ inches by 8 inches (5.5 cm by 20 cm), but it depends on the thickness of the glass, so bring the can along.

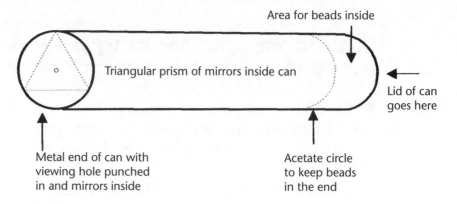

Layout of the kaleidoscope.

Procedure

1. First have the children form a triangle of the mirrors, with the reflective side facing in. Help them tape the mirrors together using masking tape. Encourage them to look down the tube of mirrors, pointing them at pictures or objects and examining the reflections. With older children, you can use this as a time to review the concepts from activity 12. Ask what angles are in the triangle and how many patterns they can see. Can they draw a connection between the number of patterns and the angles? They should see a pattern of six triangles because the triangle is equilateral and therefore each angle is 60 degrees. Have them try holding a finger at the end of the tube while looking through the tube.

2. Next they slide the mirrors into the chip can all the way down to the metal end. They may need to stuff some tissue between mirrors and can to keep the mirrors from rattling. Looking down into the tube, the mirror triangle should look like the illustration on page 78 of the activity sheet.

3. Next have each child place the chip can on the transparency and trace a circle around the end of the can. The children will cut the circles out about ⅛ inch (3 mm) smaller than the circle line so that it will fit inside the can. They need to leave tabs on the circle for taping, as shown in the illustration on page 78 of the activity sheet. They can draw these tabs on before cutting or simply cut the circle out, cutting the tabs as they go. Make sure each child sees the illustration and understands the need to leave the tabs and to cut the circle slightly smaller before he or she begins cutting.

4. After cutting out their circles, the children should fold the tabs and push the circle into the can, on top of the mirrors, with the tabs sticking up. They should adjust the circle as necessary, perhaps cutting it even smaller if it doesn't fit. They then tape the tabs to the inside walls of the can with transparent tape.

5. Next the children put the beads in the can, on top of the acetate circle, and attach the lid. The beads will rest on top of the acetate, which will keep them from falling into the mirrored part of the kaleidoscope. If you used purse mirrors, and had to cut the can short, you will need to tape on the lid.

The beads can be changed any time. Experiment with combinations of beads in many colors or with other colorful objects! You will always want a fair amount of beads as only the middle of the triangular tube will be seen at any one time, so you don't want most of the beads sliding out of sight.

Suggestions

- Encourage children to recognize the six triangles together with the 60-degree angles in the pattern as they look into the kaleidoscope.

- This activity can be done for the pure pleasure of creating the kaleidoscope, or with a review of as much of the mathematics from the previous investigation as is desired.

- It is not absolutely necessary to do the previous activity before creating the kaleidoscope, but it may make it more mathematically interesting and easier to understand. Be sure to identify the sixths going around each rotational section as you look into the can. Comparing the angles seen in other commercially available kaleidoscopes can be interesting too. Remember the angle is the number of rotational sections seen divided into 360.

Assessment

The finished product should speak for itself!

Extension Activity

The children could decorate the outside of their tubes with a tessellation design (see activity 8, page 42). Challenge them to figure out what size initial square they must choose so the shape exactly lines up with itself going around the can. The key is that the side length of the initial tessellation square must be an exact fraction of the circumference of the can for the tessellation pattern to meet up with itself going around the can.

13 ─ Kaleidoscope Activity Sheet

In this activity, you will create your very own kaleidoscope!

① First tape your three mirrors together, with the mirrors facing inward. Have fun looking through the triangular tube and recognizing the patterns. How many patterns do you see? What angle is in the triangle? What is the connection between the number of patterns and the triangle angle?

② Now slide your mirrors down inside the chip can, stuffing with a bit of tissue if necessary between the mirrors and the can so the mirrors won't rattle. If you look into the can, it should look like the illustration below.

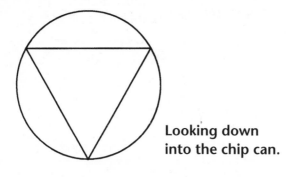

Looking down into the chip can.

③ Now trace a circle around the end of the can onto the transparency. You will cut out this circle about ⅛ inch (3 mm) smaller than your line (so it will fit in the can), but before you cut, be sure to leave four tabs on the circle as shown in the illustration at right. You can draw these on first, or just be sure to leave four tabs as you cut. Fold the tabs up and test that the circle will slide neatly into the can, with the tabs folded up.

The transparency circle with four tabs to fold up and tape to the inside of the can.

④ Slide the circle into the can, down on top of the mirrors, with the tabs folded up. Tape the tabs to the inside of the can using transparent tape. This circle keeps the beads from falling into the mirrors.

⑤ Now all you have to do is fill the end of the can with beads and attach the lid. If your can is cut off at the end, you will need to tape on the lid. Look through the hole your teacher has punched in the metal end. Be sure to look through everyone's kaleidoscope. No two are ever the same!

You can change your beads at any time, and even use other colorful objects. Experiment with combinations! Elastic, string, paper clips, or a penny might add to your designs.

Big Ideas for Small Mathematicians, 2007 © Zephyr Press

CRAWLING AROUND THE MOEBIUS STRIP

The **BIG** Idea

Turning flat objects into three-dimensional ones can give unexpected results. Just ask a topologist!

Content Areas in This Activity
Three-dimensional visualization

Process Skills Used in This Activity
- Reasoning
- Hypothesizing
- Problem solving

Prerequisite Knowledge and Skills
None

Age Appropriateness

It is useful to precut the strips for younger children, but other than that this challenge can be put to children of even primary age. It is often not the oldest who thinks of twisting the strip first! Younger children will need help taping the strip in place. They also may have more trouble making the lengthwise cuts for the extension activity.

Mathematical Idea

The branch of mathematics called *topology* is all about shapes and surfaces and dimensions. It has been said that a topologist is a mathematician who doesn't know the difference between a doughnut and a cup. That is because topologically, they are both equivalent. That means they have the same number of surfaces and the same number of holes. You can verify this with clay: You can mold a doughnut into a cup without punching any new holes!

A Moebius strip (named after a German mathematician) is a two-dimensional object with a twist in the third dimension. This twist gives the paper some neat properties, as this activity will demonstrate. The paper now has only one side! The trick to turning the paper strip into a Moebius band is to hold one end of the strip in each hand, and then turn one hand upside down before joining the loop. This will join one side of the paper strip to the other.

Experimenting with the Moebius strip.

79

☞ Theoretically, we can do the same thing by constructing a three-dimensional bottle and twisting it into the fourth dimension so that it has no inside or outside. This object is called a *Klein bottle,* after another mathematician. It might be fun and interesting to search the web using the key phrase "Klein bottle" to show kids images of this fascinating object.

HELPFUL TERMS

Edge: An *edge* is the straight line that bounds a closed shape. For flat shapes, we usually call these *sides,* but in three dimensions we call them edges. For example, a cube has 12 edges—think of it as the number of toothpicks it would take to construct it.

Moebius strip: A *Moebius strip* is a strip of paper (a two-dimensional object) with a twist in the third dimension that enables the back to meet the front—it has just one side.

Three dimensional: A *three-dimensional* object isn't flat but uses up space (volume). For example, a square is two dimensional but a cube is three dimensional.

Topology: A branch of mathematics that deals with surfaces and holes in the surfaces is called *topology.* Objects such as a doughnut and a cup are considered topologically similar because they have the same number of holes.

Two dimensional: A flat shape (you could draw it on a piece of paper), or a shape with no thickness, is *two dimensional.*

Crawling around the Moebius Strip: Making It Work

Objectives

Children will gain initial experience with the intrigue of topology.

Materials

- ✔ long narrow strip of paper, at least 2" x 2' (5 cm x 60 cm), for each child
- ✔ transparent tape for each child
- ✔ scissors for each child (optional)
- ✔ two colors of markers for each child
- ✔ small plastic turtle, bug, or other animal (optional)
- ✔ photocopy of Crawling around the Moebius Strip Activity Sheet (on page 83) for each child

Preparation

Cut the paper strips in advance.

Procedure

1. Most children will naturally pick up the strip off the table and begin to play with it. If they do not, you could model this by picking it up and examining it, asking, "Now, how could we get the turtle to the other side without going over the edge?" If you don't use a turtle or other toy animal, you could use an eraser or simply challenge the kids to draw a line on both sides of the strip without lifting up the marker, as described on the activity sheet.

2. Encourage the children to play with the paper to find a layout that the turtle (or bug, or whatever small animal you choose) can fully traverse. The turtle can only go over edges that are joined to the strip (such as an edge taped to the strip), but not over any sharp edges, such as the sides or the end if it's not joined to the strip. Have the children draw a line behind the turtle with a marker. Ultimately, they want to be able to draw the line behind the turtle all around both sides of the strip to where the turtle started without picking up the marker. So their first line will extend the length of one side of the strip only. Now, how to get the line to cross to the other side is the challenge!

3. The trick is to hold one end of the paper in each hand, and then flip one side upside down so the side that has a marker line meets the blank side, and tape it in place. Once the kids have figured it out, they can test it by drawing all around it with the other marker in a different color.

Suggestions

The first stab at a solution for many will be bending one end of the strip over and sticking it down in the middle of the strip, as the child is doing in the photograph below. This is on the right track, but the strip would have to be continuously rearranged to get into the middle of this loop. You might prompt with "That's the right idea, but how can we change it so the bug can get into the loop? The shape has to stay the same and still allow it to crawl everywhere."

Assessment

The children can self-assess the success of their strip by testing it with the marker line. If it meets up with itself on both sides of the strip, they have created a Moebius strip.

Encourage the children to pick up the strip and play with it three dimensionally.

The untwisted loop.

A half twist in the loop creates the Moebius strip.

Extension Activity

The extension of this activity is to predict what would happen if we cut the strip along the length, following the marker line down the middle. Ask them to predict what they think will happen, then pierce the strip and cut along the line drawn down the length. It's important that they pierce the strip instead of cutting from the edge. Folding the strip is a good way to start the cut in the middle of the band.

Have them test their new strip with the marker, drawing along the middle of the strip again. Ask what they think will happen if they cut it again, following the new line down the middle. Will the result be the same? Try it—the result may surprise you. But that's topology! Note: You will need a reasonably wide initial strip to be able to cut it twice lengthwise, and this part will be harder for younger children.

Crawling around the Moebius Strip Activity Sheet

14

This will get you all turned around! Can you draw a line on both sides of the paper strip without lifting your marker?

1 Start with a strip of paper and a marker. Your goal is to draw a line around the strip without lifting your marker and without going over a sharp edge. In other words, you can go over an edge that is joined to another, but not over the edge from one side to the other.

> It might help to imagine a turtle or bug walking along your strip, leaving a line behind it, as shown in the picture below. Because the turtle can't crawl over any sharp edges, it can't get to the other side. The turtle can't fly either!

2 Another rule is that you must be able to draw the line all the way around without changing the shape of the strip. You can play with the shape to find one that works now, but once you start drawing the line, you can't keep changing the shape as you draw. The line must continue until you end up back where you started.

> Pick up your paper from the table and work with it three dimensionally.

3 Once you have found out what to do, you can tape your shape in place and test it with a new color of marker. You've figured it out if you are able to go along both sides and end up where you started without lifting the marker.

Imagine a turtle crawling along the strip, leaving a line behind it.

WHAT COLOR?

Activity 15

The **BIG** Idea

Visualizing the three-dimensional shape from the two-dimensional outside surface can be a challenge!

Content Areas in This Activity
- Geometric patterning
- Three-dimensional visualization
- Nets
- Geometric terminology (optional)

Process Skills Used in This Activity
- Reasoning
- Hypothesizing (optional)
- Problem solving

Prerequisite Knowledge and Skills
Nets as surface area (helpful)

Age Appropriateness

This activity can be modified to fit various ages. Coloring simple diagrams, such as those in the illustration on the activity sheet (page 89), will be possible for most children, but creating the nets is harder. A systematic investigation of the extension activity would be more appropriate for slightly older children, such as nine- and ten-year-olds.

Mathematical Idea

The flat piece of paper needed to form an object such as a cube is called a *net*. For example, the net for a cube consists of six squares, each joined on at least one edge. There are many such arrangements that will fold up to form a cube, and figuring out all of them—and how we know we have all of them—is the extension problem for this activity.

The nets in the main part of this activity form a little house, made from four wall squares, one floor square, two roof squares, and two roof (equilateral) triangles. The four roof parts are to be one color, the rest another. Figuring out what to color each part on the flat net is part of the challenge of this activity.

There are two important mathematical skills at work here. The first is the idea that nets of shapes or polygons will sometimes fold up to make specific closed objects, such as a cube, or in this case a house. Depending on the object, more than one arrangement may be possible. So we have the spatial reasoning (that is, three-dimensional visualization) skill of seeing how the nets fold up without actually folding them, and then the hypothesizing skill of deducing whether we have all possible arrangements of pieces to make a given object. The packaging industry makes use of these skills, as do many other businesses.

The paper house for use in the activity.

HELPFUL TERMS

Area: *Area* is the number of 1 x 1 squares that it takes to cover a surface. For example, the area of a 2-inch by 3-inch rectangle is 6 square inches (that is, 2 x 3 = 6); in other words, it takes six 1-inch by 1-inch squares to cover it.

Conservation of area: This term refers to the idea that if you arrange sections of an area differently, the total area (the sum of the areas of the pieces) remains the same.

Edge: An *edge* is the straight line that bounds a closed shape. For flat shapes, we usually call these *sides,* but in three dimensions we call them edges. For example, a cube has 12 edges—think of it as the number of toothpicks it would take to construct it.

Face: The flat outside surfaces of a three-dimensional solid are *faces.* For example, a cube has six faces.

Hypothesize: Another name for *hypothesize* is *conjecture.* It means to put forth an unproven theory for testing.

Net: A layout of flat faces that fold up into a particular three-dimensional object is called a *net.* For example, you can arrange six squares into a number of nets that will fold up to construct a cube.

Proof: A mathematical *proof* is a sequence of logical deductions to establish the truth of something new from something we know. If the proof applies to an idea that includes an infinite number of values, then examples are not enough to prove something. More recently, arguments that show an idea by moving through the range of possibilities (say, with a diagram on a computer) are being considered as close to mathematical proofs, often dubbed *dynamic proofs.*

Three dimensional: A *three-dimensional* object isn't flat but uses up space (volume). For example, a square is two dimensional but a cube is three dimensional.

Two dimensional: A flat shape (you could draw it on a piece of paper), or a shape with no thickness, is *two dimensional.*

Chapter 15

What Color: Making It Work

Objectives

- Children will practice their three-dimensional visualization skills.
- Children will use problem-solving skills to investigate nets.

Materials

- ✔ half a sheet of 8 ½" x 11" red and half a sheet of 8 ½" x 11" blue paper to create a model of the house
- ✔ red crayon for each child
- ✔ blue crayon for each child
- ✔ three to five sheets of 8 ½" x 11" paper for each child
- ✔ scissors for each child
- ✔ pencil for each child
- ✔ transparent tape
- ✔ photocopy of What Color? Activity Sheet (on pages 88–89) for each child

Preparation

Construct a model house out of paper, using red for the roof and gables and blue for the walls and floor. You can use one of the templates on page 89, color it, and fold it up, or you can use different colors of construction paper.

Instead of using paper for your model house, you could use red and blue blocks, or plain wooden blocks that you paint.

Procedure

1. First show the kids the model house and explain that the illustrations on their activity sheet (page 89) will fold up to make the house. Explain that these are called *nets*.

2. Point out that the model house has red roof pieces, blue walls, and a blue floor. Have the children color in the nets to match the model. Tell them they need to figure out which parts of the net will form the roof and color those parts red. They color the walls and floor blue.

Most children will be able to see or guess the colors of the nets on page 89, but for those who have trouble with this or other nets you create, it might help to walk them through the model. Start with a face the child can locate on both the model and the net, then rotate the model, asking, "Which part of the net would be this next one?" Continue as necessary, turning the model and comparing it to the net. The two triangles must of course be red, but because they are equilateral, it may be hard to determine which edges are adjacent to the roof parts and which to the walls.

3. After they finish coloring in the nets, they can check their work by cutting them out and folding them up.

4. Then the children create their own nets, using the pattern pieces on page 89 to trace onto paper. They can test their nets, as above, by cutting them out and folding them up.

5. The children can trade nets and see if their friends can color in the correct parts blue or red.

Suggestions

- You can make this activity harder by creating some nets with the right number of pieces that do not fold up to the desired shape, mixing these in with those that do. Ask the children to determine which ones will work.

- This activity could be used in the context of a study of nets and surface area. The children should notice that the surface area stays the same for all successful nets because the same pieces are used.

Assessment

Children should have an improved facility for identifying correct nets after doing this activity.

Extension Activity

Challenge the children to find all possible nets that will fold up to make a cube. Ask them how they will know for sure when they have found them all. It might help to have six cut-out squares for each of them to work with and move around. This activity is an introduction to the nature of dynamic proof. Using moving pieces may help show that they have systematically considered all arrangements. Starting with a cube net works well because locating all nets even for a cube that has all square faces can be quite challenging. If the nets are drawn flat on the page, and we do not allow them to be moved around or flipped over, there are eleven nets that work. Finding all of them would be a challenging activity for a ten- or eleven-year-old.

What Color? Activity Sheet

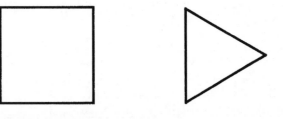

The house for this activity.

As you are working, you may want to use the model of the house. Turn the house in your hand and try to visualize the flat pattern folding up to form a shape like the model.

The little house above is painted outside in two colors on your teacher's model. The roof is red and all the other five square surfaces including the bottom are blue. Can you look at the patterns on page 2 of your activity sheet and see the house? Can you create patterns like these that will also fold up into a house?

1 First look at the patterns on the following page and try to imagine them cut out and folded up to look like the model house. These patterns are called *nets*. Nets are two-dimensional versions of the outside surfaces of three-dimensional shapes. They are what a shape would look like unfolded. Your job is to determine which parts of these nets should be red (that is, which parts will fold up to be a part of the roof) and which should be blue (that is, which will fold up into the walls and floor).

2 When you think you've figured it out, you can color in each part the right color. Check your work by cutting out the shape and folding it up.

3 After you've figured out the right colors for the nets, it's time to create your own. Using the pattern pieces below to trace onto paper, create as many nets as you can that will fold up to make the house. Test them by folding if you are not sure. Trade nets with your friends, and have them try to color them in without folding them up. See how many you can find! Can you hypothesize how many there could be?

Pattern pieces for the net.

(continued on next page)

What Color? Activity Sheet

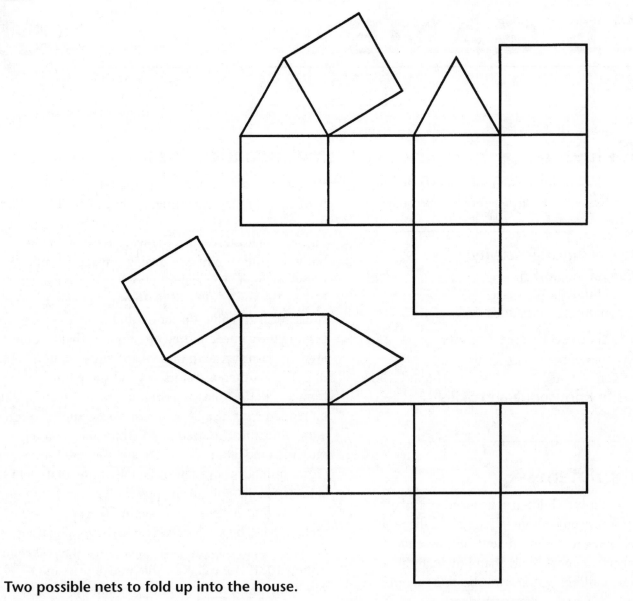

Two possible nets to fold up into the house.

BALLOONS AND DICE GAME

Activity

16

The **BIG** Idea

Mathematics gives lots of interesting and unexpected results in games. Probability . . . you just can't be sure about it!

Content Areas in This Activity
- Addition, single digit
- Probability: sample space
- Probability: combinations

Process Skills Used in This Activity
- Hypothesizing
- Problem solving

Prerequisite Knowledge and Skills
None

Age Appropriateness

This is a great game for children who need practice in single-digit addition, even without talking about the probable outcomes. Playing it multiple times will show children that some numbers are more likely than others. By about age eight or nine, children will start to be able to understand the idea of the possible combinations.

Mathematical Idea

Probability is an interesting and relatively new area of mathematics that has influence over everything from the outcomes of games to the insurance business. In the rolling of a single die, each of the six numbers is equally likely, but when the sum of two dice is considered, unexpected things happen. The sum of two dice can range from 2 to 12 (so the probability of getting a 1 is zero). But some sums seem to come up more often. For example, when playing the game, children often notice that 7 comes up a lot. The easiest way to understand the situation is to use dice of two different colors, say red and white. A 7 results from any of the following combinations: 1 on white and 6 on red; 2 on white and 5 on red; 3 on white and 4 on red; 4 on white and 3 on red; 5 on white and 2 on red; and 6 on white and 1 on red. There are six possibilities in all. Other numbers have fewer combinations that yield their sum. If you list out all the possibilities for each number, you will find 36 possible rolls in all. (This is called the *sample space,* by the way.) So the chances of getting a sum of 7 are 6 out of 36, or $\frac{1}{6}$. This is called the *probability* of rolling a 7. If you calculate the probabilities of all 36 possible outcomes, you will find they add up to 1.

The game in this activity has children using pennies (or game tokens) to represent balloons in a carnival game. On a sheet of paper marked with a row of numbers, 1 through 12, they set out their "balloons" based on their guess of which numbers will come up on the dice most often. Each time a number is rolled, they get to pop a balloon next to that number (that is, remove a penny from that number). Winning the game to follow is most likely if the balloons are clustered around the middle numbers, much like the distribution of possible outcomes. But it's more fun to play before you know this!

Possible layouts for starting to play the game.

HELPFUL TERMS

Probability: The branch of mathematics that has to do with predicting the likelihood of events is called *probability*. For example, when we roll a die, the probability of rolling a 6 on a single roll is $1/6$. There are six possibilities, all equally likely, so each will come up one sixth of the time.

Sample space: In probability, the list of all underlying possibilities, often with equal probability of occurring, is called a *sample space* (not to be confused with the *outcomes* of an experiment). For example, if we roll two dice, and the outcome is the sum of the two faces, then there are 36 possible points in the sample space, all equally likely (with probability $1/36$), but there are 11 possible outcomes (the numbers from 2 to 12). The probability of each outcome is calculated with reference to the sample space. For example, the probability of a 4 is $3/36 = 1/12$.

Sum: *Sum* is a name for the number you get when you add two or more numbers. For example, the sum of $2 + 5 + 1$ is equal to 8.

Chapter 16

Balloon and Dice Game: Making It Work

Objectives

Children will gain initial experience with probability outcomes and sample space.

Materials

- ✔ 12 pennies or game chips per child
- ✔ pair of dice per pair or trio playing the game (each die in a pair a different color)
- ✔ sheet of paper with the numbers 1 through 12 listed (as on the activity sheet) for each child
- ✔ photocopy of the Balloons and Dice Game Activity Sheet (on page 94) for each child

Preparation

Prepare each paper with the numbers 1 to 12 listed from left to right in stalls, as shown on the activity sheet on page 94.

Procedure

1. Set the stage by telling the children they are at a fair and are about to play the balloons and dice game. Tell them to pretend that the pennies (or tokens) are balloons. The sheet of paper is a wall with 12 different stalls, each marked 1 through 12.

2. Tell them that they can place the balloons under any of the stalls. They can put as many balloons as they like under a particular number, or no balloons at all. At this point, you don't need to explain anything about probability or sample space or even the fact that the numbers they choose represent guesses. Let them play the game first to get a feel for it.

3. To play, each child takes a turn rolling the dice. Whoever has a balloon beneath the number that matches the sum of the dice gets to pop that balloon (that is, remove it from the paper). The first child to pop ten balloons (with two balloons left) wins.

4. After all groups have played a few games, discuss the fact that the balloons represent guesses of what sums will appear. Ask them if some numbers came up more often than others. Ask if they think they can predict the best arrangement of balloons. Then have them play the game again.

☞ —

Allow as much experimentation as possible before discussing the sample space. Asking probing questions, such as "How many different rolls would have a sum of 7?" might start children thinking about the solution. The sample space shows all the possible combinations of rolls, and this makes clear what sums are the most likely.

5. After the children have played a few games, and when (and if) you feel they are ready, you can discuss the concept of *sample space* (unless the children are young, in which case they can continue enjoying the game and learning about the basics of probability just by observing and guessing numbers). The sample space for this game (that is, all possible roll combinations) is detailed in the chart below.

Sample Space
Possible Rolls: white die, red die

Sum	2	3	4	5	6	7	8	9	10	11	12
	1,1	1,2	1,3	1,4	1,5	1,6	2,6	3,6	4,6	5,6	6,6
		2,1	3,1	5,1	6,1	6,2	6,3	6,4	6,5		
			2,2	2,3	2,4	2,5	3,5	4,5	5,5		
				3,2	4,2	5,2	5,3	5,4			
					3,3	3,4	4,4				
						4,3					

Suggestions

- This game is a great environment for simply practicing single-digit addition, even without examining probability.
- Children may notice right away that a sum of 1 is impossible, or they may get stuck on this idea and put a penny on 1, then find they can't remove it during the course of a game.

Assessment

- Children can apply the concept of sample space to other contexts, and they show an understanding of sample space in the numbers they choose in this game.
- Assess young children based on their ability to total the sum of dice with each roll.

Extension Activity

Have the children track the long-term outcomes of several games by making a master chart and putting an "x" under each number every time that sum occurs. After a while, they will have a graph of the most likely outcomes. Challenge them to explain the shape of the graph from the numbers on the chart. (The shapes will get more similar to the shape of the numbers on the chart the more games they track.) What does it say about probability?

Balloons and Dice Game
Activity Sheet

Imagine you are at the fair and want to play the following game. You get to put 12 balloons anywhere you want on the wall in the stalls marked 1 to 12, which are arranged in a line. There are several stalls, so you can play against several friends, each of you with your own row of balloons. Here is one possible arrangement of 12 balloons:

Each number is a stall, and each circle is a balloon.

① Get into a group and each of you set your pennies (or tokens) under any numbers you choose on your sheet of paper. Remember, the pennies are your balloons, and the numbers are the stalls.

② Each player takes a turn rolling two dice. If you have a balloon on the number that matches the sum of a roll, you can pop one balloon there (remove a penny). For example, if you roll a 3 and a 6, you can pop one of the balloons in stall 9. (You may only pop the balloon that is the sum of the two dice.) The first player who pops 10 balloons (with two balloons left) is the winner.

③ Play the game a few times to get the feel of it. Do some numbers seem to come up more than others? How can you predict the best initial arrangement of balloons?

BALANCES AND EQUATIONS

The **BIG** Idea

Equations . . . what a balancing act! The equals sign means the balance is level.

Content Areas in This Activity
- Addition, single digit
- Subtraction, single digit
- Addition, double digit
- Multiplication, single digit (optional)
- Division, single-digit divisor (optional)

Process Skills Used in This Activity
- Reasoning
- Problem solving
- Concept of proof (optional)

Prerequisite Knowledge and Skills
- Addition, single digit
- Subtraction, single digit
- Multiplication, single digit (helpful)
- Division, single-digit divisor (helpful)

Age Appropriateness

Younger children may need help constructing the balance, but all children will enjoy playing with it. Choose numbers based on the children's numeracy understanding.

Mathematical Idea

The elementary curriculum topic of patterning and algebra allows children to experience creating and generalizing patterns of their own. These patterns can yield linear relationships, which require equation-solving skills.

Students are often afraid of solving equations. One of the reasons for this fear may be an inadequate grasp of the concrete idea behind the allowable operations. Indeed, even secondary-level students may find the "what you do to one side you must do to the other" rule confusing.

The balance is a concrete metaphor for an equation. The equals sign means the balance must stay level. Children can learn firsthand that to keep it balanced you must always do the same thing to both sides, for example "remove one from both sides" or "take half of each side." Playing with various weights on a balance can be a fun (and very useful) mathematical activity.

An easy-to-make balance.

HELPFUL TERMS

Algebra: *Algebra* refers to rules and language for working with mathematical symbols, such as those that stand for unknown quantities or geometric objects.

Divisibility: The *divisibility* of a number describes whether any numbers can be divided into it with no remainder. For example, 10, 15, and 20 are divisible by 5. The divisibility rule for 5 is that 5 will divide evenly (with no remainder) into numbers that end in 5 or 0.

Equation: A mathematical statement with an equals sign that shows that two quantities have the same measure is called an *equation*. It may include unknown quantities. For example, $9 + 1 = 2 \times 5$ is an equation, and so is $2x = 10$.

Factors: Numbers that divide evenly (with no remainder) into a number are *factors* of that number (see also *divisibility*).

Level: *Level* means flat or parallel to the floor, as in a balanced, or equally weighted, scale.

Sum: *Sum* is a name for the number you get when you add two or more numbers. For example, the sum of $2 + 5 + 1$ is equal to 8.

Balances and Equations: Making It Work

Objectives

Children will model linear equations concretely.

Materials

- ✔ two small yogurt cups for each pair
- ✔ 5' (1 ½ m) twine for each pair
- ✔ scissors for each pair
- ✔ tape for each pair
- ✔ colorful markers for each pair (optional)
- ✔ paper towel tube for each pair
- ✔ several pennies for each pair
- ✔ hole punch to pass around (or pointed scissors to use with adult help)
- ✔ two sheets of tissue for each pair
- ✔ balls for weights made from clay for each pair, for example:
  - yellow balls weighing one penny
  - blue balls weighing 2 pennies
  - red balls weighing 3 pennies
- ✔ photocopy of the Balances and Equations Activity Sheet (pages 100–101) for each child

Preparation

- You may need to construct the balance in advance, using the directions below. Alternatively, you could use commercial balances instead of making them.

- Prepare the weights in advance so that the clay balls of each color weigh exactly one, two, and three pennies, as described above. You can weigh these using a commercial balance, or make a balance in advance for this purpose and to use as an example for the kids.

Procedure

1. First have the children get into pairs, then get them started making the balance (unless you decide to make these ahead of time). Have them begin by cutting the twine into three equal pieces.

2. Next have them make a small hole near each end of the paper towel tube (each hole should be on the same side of the tube, not one on top and one on bottom). A hole punch works best, but an adult can help make the holes with pointed scissors.

3. Next have them thread a piece of twine through each hole, pulling each piece through the end of the tube, so that both ends of the twine hang down on each side.

4. Now the children make two holes in each yogurt cup on opposite sides near the rim, then tie an end of the twine through each hole. Alternatively, they could just tape the twine securely on either side of the cup.

5. Next, they tie the third piece of twine to the center of the tube. They will use this to suspend the balance. If the tube doesn't balance exactly, have them slide the twine back and forth until it does. Then have them hold the twine in place with tape. Double-check that each balance is balanced.

6. They can decorate the balances if they wish using markers. For example, it might be fun to put a big equals sign on the tube. Now they are ready to start modeling equations.

7. Hand out the pennies and clay balls to each group and let them play awhile with their balances, putting different items in either side to see what will balance. Explain that their balances will be level when the weight on each side is the same, is *equal*. Then explain that keeping the balances level will be the rule for the games that follow. They will always be trying to make their balances level.

8. Have one person in each pair put pennies in one side of the balance only, without letting the other see how many he or she has put in. The child should then put the tissue over the cup, just to hide the contents without adding weight. Explain that the pennies in that cup are an unknown quantity.

9. The other child in the pair tries to guess how many pennies are in the hidden side by putting pennies into the other until the balance is level. At that point they will have an equal number of pennies on each side, an equal weight. Now have them switch so that the other child puts pennies in for his or her partner to guess.

10. Next have the children use their balance to solve an equation. Tell them to put a ball *and some pennies* in one cup. They will then put only pennies in the other cup until the balance is level; that is, until the weight is equal on both sides.

11. Ask them if they can figure out how many pennies the ball equals in weight. They can add or take away pennies from either side. The illustration on the activity sheet (page 101) gives them a clue of how to go about this. In that example, they have a clay ball and three pennies on one side, and they have to add five pennies to the other side for balance. To figure out the weight of the ball (in pennies), they first have to isolate the ball on one side, which means removing the three pennies on that side. Removing these pennies makes the balance uneven, so they have to do the exact same thing to the other side—remove three pennies. That leaves the ball on one side and two pennies on the other. That means the ball is equal in weight to two pennies. This is a good time to talk about the concept that whatever you do to one side of a level balance, you have to do to the other side to keep it level; in other words, to keep both sides equal.

12. Enjoy making up your own equations for the children to solve. They could try to find how many pennies each ball equals, then try to find how many pennies two of each ball equals, and so on. They may need to be reminded of the rule that the balance must always stay level or balanced.

Discourage students from using a trial-and-error method by insisting on the rule that the balance must stay level at all times. To do this, they must repeat the same action on both sides when adding or subtracting.

Suggestions

- You can make up and solve all sorts of simple equations using the balance. It is not necessary to write out the solution algebraically at this stage, but the activity will provide a concrete understanding of the algebraic process when it comes later.

- You could encourage older children to write out the mathematical operations as they perform them. This will prove a solid introduction to the skill of solving linear equations.

- Encourage children to make up their own games.

Assessment

Children can demonstrate their understanding by solving an example.

Extension Activity

You can make a harder game by having the children use two of the same object on one side, and the right number of pennies to balance on the other side. They can still add pennies to each side, but they need to be sure they begin with it balanced and always keep it that way. Have the children model any simple linear equation, such as $2x + 1 = 5$, as illustrated below.

The ball in the illustration below is the unknown quantity, the x.

$$\bigcirc \quad \bigcirc \quad \bigcirc \; = \; \bigcirc \quad \bigcirc \quad \bigcirc \quad \bigcirc \quad \bigcirc$$

First they would need to remove one penny from each side (making the equation $4 = 2x$), and then to get the ball weight, they would divide each side by 2, which means removing half of the contents of each cup, leaving one ball on one side and two pennies on the other, proving that x (the ball) equals 2 (the weight of two pennies).

Balances and Equations
Activity Sheet

For this activity, you get to make a balance. You can use it to play with different weights. Always keep your balance level. The balance is a model of a mathematical equation, and you will be practicing the techniques of solving equations.

1 Get into pairs and cut your piece of twine into three equal pieces.

2 Now make a small hole near each end of the paper towel tube (each hole should be on the same side of the tube, not one on top and one on bottom).

3 Next, thread a piece of twine through each hole and out each end of the tube so that you have two pieces hanging down on each side.

4 Now make two holes on opposite sides of each yogurt cup and tie one end of the twine through each hole, or securely tape the string to each side near the rim of the cup.

5 Tie a piece of twine around the center of the tube to suspend your balance. If the cups don't balance exactly, you need to slide the twine back and forth a bit until they do. When the balance is level, hold the twine in place with a piece of tape.

6 Now decorate your balance with markers. For example, you could put a large equals sign (=) on your tube.

7 Play around with putting the balls of clay and the pennies in the cups. For example, if you put four pennies in each side, and now remove only one from one side, what happens? What if you remove one penny from each side instead? When you have the same number (or weight) in each cup, the balance should be level, which means the tube should be straight horizontally, not tipped. This will be the rule for the games you will play—the balance must always be level.

8 For the first game, one of you puts pennies in one side of the balance only, without letting the other see how many, then puts a piece of tissue over the cup to cover it. The other person tries to guess how many pennies are in that cup by adding pennies to the other cup to make the balance level. After the second person figures out the number of pennies, switch roles and try it again.

Big Ideas for Small Mathematicians, 2007 © Zephyr Press

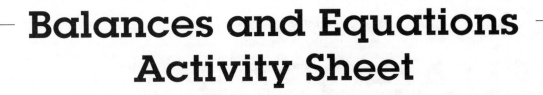

9 The next game makes things more interesting. This time, one of you puts a clay ball (which is equal in weight to an exact number of pennies) in one cup along with a few pennies, and the number of pennies with the same weight in the other cup. You will know the pennies are the same weight when your balance is level.

10 Can you figure out how many pennies the ball's weight equals? How would you figure this out? Remember, you can add or take away pennies from either cup, but you still want to keep your balance level. The illustration below shows an example. In the illustration, we have a ball and three pennies on one side and five pennies on the other side. If we take away three pennies from both sides, we have just the ball on one side and the two pennies on the other side. In other words, we've *isolated* the ball. Now we can see that the weight of one ball equals two pennies.

11 Can you figure out how many pennies are equal in weight to a different ball and some pennies in your balance? What can you do to always keep your balance level?

> Remember that in the example, when we took three pennies from one side, we took three pennies from the other side as well to keep the balance level.

12 Have fun figuring out the weights of all the balls, or try to solve the games (equations) your teacher gives you. You could even make up your own!

Removing three pennies from each side isolates the clay ball (the larger circle).

PROOF WITH PYTHAGORAS AND FERMAT

Activity 18

The **BIG** Idea

Sometimes it's hard to be sure of a mathematical idea. At what point do we know something will always be true?

Content Areas in This Activity

- Addition, single digit
- Addition, double digit
- Multiplication, single digit
- Square numbers
- Angle measurement
- Volume measurement
- Geometric terminology (optional)

Process Skills Used in This Activity

- Reasoning
- Problem solving
- Hypothesizing
- Concept of proof

Prerequisite Knowledge and Skills

- Multiplication, single digit
- Idea of area of squares

Age Appropriateness

Children may do either or both parts of the activity. Most children will be able to do the first part, but children may need to be at least eight years old for the second part. Older children (about age ten) will be able to see the more algebraic interpretation and do calculations of other examples without constructing the areas and volumes.

Mathematical Idea

The Pythagorean theorem has been around for thousands of years. A group of mathematicians called the Pythagorean Brotherhood, named after their leader, Pythagoras, came up with the idea. They were reported to put members to death who told any of their secrets!

One of these secrets was the discovery that if you measure and add the areas of the squares on two sides of a right-angled triangle (the kind with a square corner), that the area of the square drawn on the third side would exactly equal the sum of the other two areas. This led to the discovery of square roots, and of the fact that not all square roots are exact numbers.

Some numbers will work exactly. For example, drawing a right angle with one side of length 3 and one 4 will give a diagonal side (called the *hypotenuse*) of length 5. The areas will be 3 x 3, or 9, and 4 x 4, or 16, on the small squares, which add up to 5 x 5, or 25, on the bigger one.

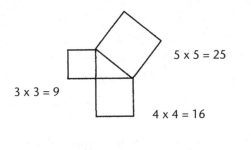

3 x 3 = 9

5 x 5 = 25

4 x 4 = 16

9 + 16 = 25

However, just looking at several examples isn't enough to be sure something is always true. For example, think of "proving" that all odd numbers are prime. Since 3, 5, and 7 are both odd and prime, we might conclude that this is true for all odd numbers, but if we hit upon the counter example of 9, we will have proved this idea to be false. A formal argument that works for *any* numbers is always the best bet. A formal proof of the Pythagorean theorem reads like an algebraic argument (see the example proof in the box at right). Many such proofs have been devised since Pythagoras's time.

It is interesting to note that if a, b, and c are the sides of a right-angled triangle, then the Pythagorean relationship only works for squaring the numbers ($a^2 + b^2 = c^2$). It does not work for the case of a + b = c because the triangle wouldn't exist. The sum of a and b must be greater than c. Nor, as we see in the second part of this activity, does the Pythagorean relationship work for cubes; that is, $a^3 + b^3 = c^3$ does not work.

There are many proofs of the Pythagorean theorem. In this activity, the children get a taste of the Pythagorean theorem without devising a formal proof. Later, often in high school, they will explore formal proofs of this theorem, such as the one below.

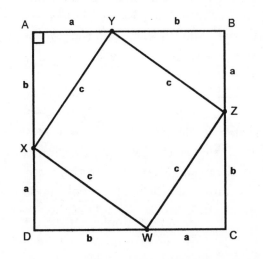

Pythagorean Proof Example

Construct square WXYZ in square ABCD. The area of ABCD is $(a + b)^2$ because a + b is the side length of ABCD. The area of ABCD is also $c^2 + 4(\frac{1}{2}ab)$; in other words, the area of WXYZ plus the four triangles.

So $(a + b)^2 = c^2 + 4(\frac{1}{2}ab)$

which can be broken down further into $a^2 + 2ab + b^2 = c^2 + 2ab$

Subtracting 2ab from each side above, we have $a^2 + b^2 = c^2$ in any right-angled triangle abc as above.

The counter example that the children construct in the second part of this activity is enough to disprove $a^3 + b^3 = c^3$. One counter example is enough to show an idea doesn't always work. Fermat's last theorem goes even further. It states that for any dimension n, there are no whole numbers a, b, and c such that $a^n + b^n = c^n$. Looking at the case of n = 3, this theorem states that there are no whole numbers for $a^3 + b^3 = c^3$, as discussed above. These numbers don't have to be the sides of a right-angled triangle for the theorem to apply. So maybe $3^3 + 4^3$ doesn't equal 5^3, but could it equal 6^3? Pierre de Fermat believed no such numbers existed. He wrote in a marginal note that he had a truly marvelous proof, but the margin was too small to contain it. He never did write out this proof, and finding it fascinated mathematicians for centuries. Finally, at the end of the twentieth century, British mathematician Andrew Wiles proved the theorem—it took him seven years!

HELPFUL TERMS

Angle: The amount of rotation needed to get from one direction to another is an *angle*. Often we speak of the angle between two lines: This is the amount of rotation needed to get from one line to the other. It is often measured in degrees (see also *degree*).

Area: *Area* is the number of 1 x 1 squares that it takes to cover a surface. For example, the area of a 2-inch by 3-inch rectangle is 6 square inches (that is, 2 x 3 = 6); in other words, it takes six 1-inch by 1-inch squares to cover it.

Cube: A three-dimensional object with six square faces is a *cube*. All the angles are 90 degrees.

Degree: A unit for measuring rotation, abbreviated as °, is a *degree*. A complete rotation is said to be 360 degrees. This comes from the historical thought that it took 360 days for the Earth to revolve once around the sun. Two lines at right angles form angles of $\frac{1}{4}$ rotation, which is 90 degrees (that is, 360 divided by 4).

Edge: An *edge* is the straight line that bounds a closed shape. For flat shapes, we usually call these *sides*, but in three dimensions we call them edges. For example, a cube has 12 edges—think of it as the number of toothpicks it would take to construct it.

Face: The flat outside surfaces of a three-dimensional solid are called *faces*. For example, a cube has six faces.

Fermat's last theorem: *Fermat's last theorem* is a result put forth by French mathematician Pierre de Fermat several hundred years ago. He observed that there are lots of examples in which the sum of two squares is a square (e.g., $3^2 + 4^2 = 5^2$ but that this can never happen for whole numbers with powers greater than 2. For example, it's never true that the sum of two cubes is a cube, when the cubes have whole-numbered sides. So $3^3 + 4^3$ does not equal 5^3 or 6^3 or cubes of any other whole numbers.

HELPFUL TERMS

Formula: An algebraic rule for getting a result is a *formula*. For example, the formula for the area of a rectangle is length x width = area.

Height: The vertical measure of an object, measured from the base to the highest point, is its *height*.

Hypotenuse: This term specifically refers to the side of a right-angled triangle that is opposite the right angle—it will be the longest side of the triangle.

Hypothesize: Another name for *hypothesize* is *conjecture*. It means to put forth an unproven theory for testing.

Length: *Length* is the measure of one dimension of a geometric object, such as one side of a rectangle.

Net: A layout of flat faces that fold up into a particular three-dimensional object is called a *net*. For example, you can arrange six squares into a number of nets that will fold up to construct a cube.

Proof: A mathematical *proof* is a sequence of logical deductions to establish the truth of something new from something we know. If the proof applies to an idea that includes an infinite number of values, then examples are not enough to prove something. More recently, arguments that show an idea by moving through the range of possibilities (say with a diagram on a computer) are being considered as close to mathematical proofs, often dubbed *dynamic proofs*.

Proof by counter example: One accepted way to prove something false is to come up with a counter example—an example for which the idea doesn't hold. This is considered enough evidence to assert that the idea doesn't always work, so it is not universally true.

Pythagorean theorem: This theorem describes the relationship of squares drawn on each of the three sides of a right-angled triangle: The areas of the two smaller squares added together will always exactly equal the square drawn on the longer side (called the *hypotenuse*).

Square numbers: *Square numbers* represent the areas of squares that have sides of whole (not fractional) numbers. For example, 25 is a square number because it is the area of a 5 x 5 square.

Sum: *Sum* is a name for the number you get when you add two or more numbers. For example, the sum of 2 + 5 + 1 is equal to 8.

Theorem: *Theorem* is a name for a mathematical idea that can be proven to be always true.

Three dimensional: A *three-dimensional* object isn't flat but uses up space (volume). For example, a square is two dimensional but a cube is three dimensional.

Triangle: A three-sided flat (plane) figure (or polygon) is called a *triangle*. A *right-angled* triangle has one 90-degree angle in it.

Two dimensional: A flat shape (you could draw it on a piece of paper), or a shape with no thickness, is *two dimensional*.

Volume: The space used by a three-dimensional shape, or the quantity of material needed to fill it, is the shape's *volume*.

Whole numbers: Numbers, such as 0, 1, 2, 3, and so forth, that do not have decimal places (other than zero) are *whole numbers*.

Width: The distance across a shape is its *width*.

Proof with Pythagoras and Fermat: Making It Work

Objectives

- Children will experiment with some famous mathematical ideas.
- Children will explore the Pythagorean theorem geometrically and discuss what they think would be enough evidence to be sure it always worked.
- Children will experience a proof by counter example of the idea that the Pythagorean theorem doesn't work in three dimensions.

Materials

- ✔ five sheets of 8½" x 11" paper for each child
- ✔ a sheet of 8½" x 11" graph paper for each child
- ✔ scissors for each child
- ✔ glue stick for each child
- ✔ ruler for each child
- ✔ pencil for each child
- ✔ several cups light cereal, rice, or foam chips for each child
- ✔ photocopy of the Proof with Pythagoras and Fermat Activity Sheet (on pages 110–111) for each child

Preparation

For younger children, or just to save time, you could preassemble the cubes for the second part of the activity.

Procedure 1: Pythagorean Theorem

1. First have children use the graph paper to draw a right-angled triangle, a triangle with a square corner.

2. Now, using their rulers, they measure the length of one side, then draw a square using that side of the triangle as one of the sides, with the other sides of the square the same length (as shown in the illustration below). They should write "A" on or next to this square. You could review the area of the square with the children at this point.

3. Have them do the same for the other sides of the triangle, labeling one square "B" and the largest square "C."

👉 **B**e sure the children really draw a square of side length c. This square is harder to see because side c is slanted on the original triangle.

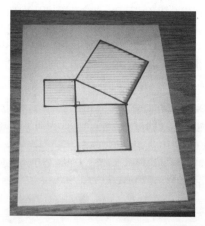

The three squares drawn on the sides of the right-angled triangle.

4. Next they pick the largest square, the one that matches up to the hypotenuse, and cut it out. Tell them they are going to check and see if the area of the big square is the same as that of the two small ones added together.

> Try both parts of the activity in a group, so everyone can examine and discuss the examples together.

5. They should cut out the next largest square and set it on top of the large one, noting that there are gaps around the smaller square where it doesn't meet up with the edges of the larger square. Do they think they can fill those gaps exactly with the smallest square?

6. Next they cut out the smallest square, then cut it more to fit the gaps. If they cut carefully, they should be able to fill the gaps so that both smaller squares cover the largest square.

7. The most important part of this activity is the discussion at this point. Looking at the various different examples, ask the children whether they think this idea will always be true. Could there be a case where it wouldn't work? Discuss how mathematicians like to have a formal logical (mathematical) argument before they are totally convinced of something. Such logical deductive arguments are called *proofs*.

8. Before starting the second part of the activity (an exploration of Fermat's last theorem), ask the kids to predict whether they think the same principle they just explored will also be true with cubes instead of squares. In other words, if they construct cubes with faces that are the length of each triangle side, will the largest cube be able to hold the same amount (will it have the same *volume*) as the two smaller cubes put together?

Procedure 2: Extending to Cubes

1. Using the same triangle from the first part of the activity, have the kids construct a cube with sides the same length as one side of the triangle. In other words, they will need five squares identical in size to square A from the first part of the activity. If you worked on activity 15 (What Color?) with the children, you could remind them that they can arrange the squares as a *net* for an open cube, as shown in the illustration on page 111.

2. Have them cut out the net, or the five squares, and assemble them into a cube that's open on top by taping the sides together.

3. They repeat the process to make cubes for the other two sides (using five squares the size of square B and five squares the size of square C from the first part of the activity). Ultimately, they should have three cubes that line up with the triangle, as shown in the photo at right.

An open cube constructed on each side of the triangle.

4. Now they fill the two smaller cubes right to the top with cereal, rice, or foam chips.

5. Next, they pour the contents of both of the smaller cubes into the larger cube. Ask them if they are able to fill up the larger cube. Discuss that by finding one example where something isn't true, they've shown that it can't always be true. In this case, they found one example where the sum of the volumes of the two smaller cubes doesn't equal the volume of the larger cube. So there isn't a version of the Pythagorean theorem with cubes instead of squares. With older kids, you can explain that they just proved something wasn't always true using proof by counter example, by finding one example where it doesn't apply. (Fermat's last theorem actually asserts a bit more; namely, that there are no whole numbers at all for which the idea $a^3 + b^3 = c^3$ works. The a, b, and c do not have to be sides of a triangle.) Younger kids can just experience the concept that the contents of the smaller cubes don't fill the larger cube (as the smaller squares filled the larger square) without needing to understand the idea of proof in depth.

Suggestions

- Children may need help constructing squares of a given size.

- Encourage discussion about whether seeing these examples proves the idea. A mathematician would say that even a huge number of examples is not a proof. The idea in the first activity does happen to be true, and a proof is often given in high school.

- Children may need a little help constructing the cubes for the second part of the activity.

- You could encourage older children to calculate the measures of the volumes of the three cubes. They should find through numerical calculations alone that the idea does not always work. For example, $(3 \times 3 \times 3) + (4 \times 4 \times 4) = 91$, which is not equal to $5 \times 5 \times 5 = 125$. This part of the activity is a proof by counter example. If you can find even one case where a theorem doesn't work, you have proved its falsity—that is, it is not always true. (But proving it is *never* true is another matter!)

Assessment

Children can discuss the difference between examples of something being true and knowing something will always be true. You might ask them what finding a counter example means: Does it mean the idea doesn't always work? Does it imply that the idea *never* works?

Extension Activity

Have the children explore whether the sum of the two smaller areas would add up to the larger area if they constructed other shapes on each side of the triangle, such as an equilateral triangle or a regular hexagon.

The Pythagorean theorem has a practical use in measuring distances. If we want to know the distance across a lake, for example, we can set up two measurements (a and b) on the shore at right angles (along the lake horizontally and vertically). Considering the distance across the lake (the hypotenuse) is equal to $a^2 + b^2$, we can calculate the distance by squaring a and b, adding them, and using a calculator to get the square root (because the square root of c^2 is c). Challenge the children to calculate the distance across the lake if a = 12 and b = 5.

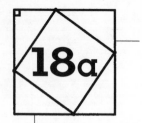

Proof with Pythagoras and Fermat Activity Sheet

18a

Pythagoras and Fermat were famous people who had interesting mathematical ideas related to geometry. Both wanted to find a way to prove their ideas were correct. In this activity, you get to explore both ideas and think about what it would take to prove either one to be true.

The Pythagorean Theorem

1 On graph paper, draw a triangle that has a square corner, just like the one below (but you can make it any size). This is called a *right-angled triangle*.

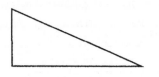

2 Now measure the length of one side with your ruler, and draw a square with all four sides of this length. Write "A" on or next to this square.

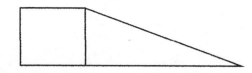

3 Do the same for the other two sides, and label the squares "B" and "C," with "C" as the largest square.

4 Pick the largest square (the one on the longest side of the triangle), cut it out, and set it in front of you.

> The longest side of a triangle is called its *hypotenuse.*

5 Now check to see if the area of the big square is the same as the areas of the two small ones added together. This is the idea that Pythagoras had (that a x a + b x b = c x c). First, put the second largest square on top of the big one. Notice that it doesn't completely cover the large square, but instead leaves gaps.

6 Now cut up the small square to fill in the gaps. If you cut carefully, you should be able to cut the smallest square into pieces that fill the gaps, so both smaller squares cover the largest square. In fact, this will work with any size right-angled triangle.

Of course this is not a proof, just one of many examples. The idea that $a^2 + b^2 = c^2$ is called the *Pythagorean theorem* and it has been around for thousands of years.

7 Discuss with your friends what you think would be needed to be sure this idea always works.

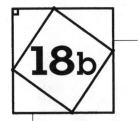

Proof with Pythagoras and Fermat Activity Sheet

Extending to Cubes

Now, if you make *cubes* on each side of the triangle, do you think the volume you need to fill the two small cubes will be the same as the amount for the large one? Fermat wondered if you could add up the volumes of two cubes with whole-number sides and get another whole-numbered cube (where the side lengths do not necessarily form a triangle). Let's try it on the triangle first and see!

1 To make the first cube (or open box, which you're going to leave open so you can fill it), you have to cut out five squares the same size as square A. Laid out, before making the cube, the squares might look like this:

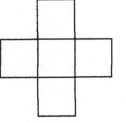

2 Now tape the five squares together to make an open cube.

3 Make open cubes on sides B and C in the same way, making the dimensions the size of each triangle side.

> The cubes will all have different heights.

4 Now let's experiment. Fill the two smaller cubes right to the top with a light material such as cereal, rice, or foam chips.

5 Pour both of the amounts from the two smaller cubes into the bigger cube. Are you able to fill the larger cube? If you can find even one example where the two small volumes don't equal the large volume, you have proved that the theorem doesn't always hold true for cubes. In other words, the sum of the two smaller volumes doesn't always equal the large volume the way the sum of the area of the smaller squares equaled the area of the largest square.

> When you can prove that something is not always true by finding just one example when it's not, this is called a *proof by counter example.*

Recently mathematician Andrew Wiles proved that the idea behind the Pythagorean theorem works only for squares, not cubes or shapes of higher dimensions. In fact, he proved that there are no whole numbers at all made into cubes for which the two smaller cubes add up to another perfect (whole-numbered) cube; nor does this work in higher dimensions. This is called Fermat's last theorem because it was the only one of Fermat's theorems no one had proved yet—until Andrew Wiles came along. It took Wiles seven years to prove!

STREAMERS PROBLEM

Activity 19

The **BIG** Idea

There are real mathematical formulas to be found by investigating fairly simple problems.

Content Areas in This Activity

- Addition, single and double digit
- Multiplication, single digit (optional)
- Division, single-digit divisor (optional)
- Geometric patterning (optional)
- Numeric patterning
- Pattern rules
- Iterative patterns

Process Skills Used in This Activity

- Reasoning
- Hypothesizing
- Problem solving
- Concept of proof (optional)
- Communication (optional)

Prerequisite Knowledge and Skills

- Addition, single and double digit
- Subtraction, single digit
- Multiplication, single digit (helpful)

Age Appropriateness

Children will need to be able to multiply to work with this problem easily. However, I recall a child who was not able to multiply but who quickly saw the method as "subtract one from the number (of dots), and then write down all the numbers going down to one, and add them up." This child was supposed to be very poor in mathematics according to her teacher. The recognition she received for solving such a difficult problem was incredibly important to her—and her school grade improved from failing to A's over the next several years! It's not always inappropriate to let children try a challenging problem for the chance to make some mathematical discoveries.

Mathematical Idea

There are many wonderful patterns in mathematics, and often a relationship seems to spring out of more than one type of pattern. In this activity, a pattern of addition, such as adding up a list of consecutive whole numbers (1 + 2 + 3 + 4 . . .), has the same solution as a pattern of multiplication and division, n (n − 1) ÷ 2, which can be also be used to add up a list of consecutive numbers from 1 to n − 1.

This activity starts with the children modeling a mathematical problem using streamers, a problem with both an additive and multiplicative solution. You start with a group of six children, then ask them how many streamers are required to connect each child to every other child once. Focusing on one child, you would ask how many streamers that child would need to hold to connect to the other five children—five. Focus on another child next and ask the same question, but this time that child is connecting to four other children, since he or she is already connected to the previous child. Continuing as such enables the children to do some true mathematical exploration by figuring out how many streamers they need to join every child to every other child in groups of varying numbers of children. Through this exploration, children learn to relate the number of streamers to the number of children in each situation, and then to relate them in general by discovering a rule to apply to every similar situation.

Using different colored streamers may help illuminate the relationship. For example, in a group of four children, you could start by giving one child three red streamers (one fewer than the number of children in the group) to connect that child to the other three children in the group. Then give the next child two blue streamers to connect to the other two children in the group (minus the first child, to whom the second child is already connected with a red streamer). Then you would give the next child one green streamer to connect with the other child in the group (minus the first two, to whom this child is already connected with one red streamer and one blue streamer). The last child in the group gets no new streamers because now all children are connected. So for four children, the solution to how many streamers are required to connect them becomes 3 (red) + 2 (blue) + 1 (green) = 6. This is called

a *recursive solution* because each number we add is based on the previous number. This is one way to look at the problem using addition.

Another way to look at this problem is to search for a pattern involving multiplication. We saw above that the number of streamers each child holds is one less than the number of children. (They are each holding a streamer to connect to every child, other than themselves.) With this in mind, can we just multiply the number of children by the number of streamers each holds, which will be one less than the number of children? For a group of four, then, we would multiply 4 x 3 for a total of 12. Oops! That's counting each streamer at both ends. So we have to divide by 2. This gives the result (4 x 3) ÷ 2 = 6, or a general rule of $n(n-1) \div 2$, where n is the number of children.

If you are lucky enough to have a group of children discover both ways of looking at the problem, encourage them to notice that they have invented a fast way to add a list of consecutive numbers from n − 1 down to 1. That is, $1 + 2 + 3 \ldots + (n-1) = n(n-1) \div 2$. Gauss invented this formula when his teacher asked him to add the numbers 1 to 100 for punishment. His formula, $n(n+1) \div 2$, is essentially the same as $n(n-1) \div 2$. The difference is in what you allow n to be. So if you wish to add 1 through 100, you could have n = 100 and use the n + 1 version, or you could have n − 1 = 100, so that n = 101, and you use the n − 1 version to achieve the same solution.

The streamers problem illustrated by five children.

HELPFUL TERMS

Algebra: *Algebra* refers to rules and language for working with mathematical symbols, such as those that stand for unknown quantities or geometric objects.

Equation: A mathematical statement with an equals sign that shows that two quantities have the same measure is called an *equation*. It may include unknown quantities. For example, 9 + 1 = 2 x 5 is an equation, and so is 2x = 10.

Formula: An algebraic rule for getting a result is a *formula*. For example, the formula for the area of a rectangle is length x width = area.

Gauss's formula: *Gauss's formula* is one he invented when asked by a teacher to add up the numbers 1 to 100 as a punishment. He added them up twice like this:

1	+	2	+	3	+	4 . . .	+	100
100	+	99	+	98	+	97 . . .	+	1

and saw that for twice the sum he had 100 pairs of sums of 101. So he calculated the sum as 100 x 101 ÷ 2. In general, the formula for the sum of numbers 1 to n is n (n + 1) ÷ 2. This is like the streamers problem for 101 kids.

Hypothesize: Another name for *hypothesize* is *conjecture*. It means to put forth an unproven theory for testing.

Iterative process: Repeating a rule over and over, possibly on a smaller or larger scale, is an *iterative process*. For example, take your calculator and enter 1,000 and hit the square root button again and again. This is an iterative process that gives a sequence of numbers converging to 1.

Patterns: Sets of items, such as numbers or shapes, that are continued in a predictable way are called *patterns*. *Linear patterns* change by the same amount each time: for example, 2, 4, 6, 8, . . . (changing by 2) or red, blue, red, blue. *Nonlinear patterns* change by a different amount each time: for example, 2, 4, 7, 11, 16, . . . (changing by 2, then 3, then 4, then 5, and so on). *Second-degree patterns* are nonlinear patterns that have a second-degree term in them, such as n^2.

Product: The result we get when multiplying two or more numbers is called a *product*. For example, multiplying 2 times 3 gives a product of 6.

Proof: A mathematical *proof* is a sequence of logical deductions to establish the truth of something new from something we know. If the proof applies to an idea that includes an infinite number of values, then examples are not enough to prove something. More recently, arguments that show an idea by moving through the range of possibilities (say with a diagram on a computer) are being considered as close to mathematical proofs, often dubbed *dynamic proofs*.

Recursive solution: A *recursive solution* involves getting the answer to a repeated process by knowing the previous term and how much the terms change each time. For example, if you know a set of numbers goes up by 3 each time, and the previous number is 11, then the next number is 11 + 3 or 14.

Sum: *Sum* is a name for the number you get when you add two or more numbers. For example, the sum of 2 + 5 + 1 is equal to 8.

Theorem: *Theorem* is a name for a mathematical idea that can be proven to be always true.

Streamers Problem: Making It Work

Objectives

- Children explore a famous mathematical problem, often known as the handshakes or nodes problem, in a concrete way. The problem is to calculate the number of connections needed to connect a group of objects each directly to each other.
- Children experience a nonlinear problem.

Materials

- ✔ five streamers of one color
- ✔ four streamers of a second color
- ✔ three streamers of a third color
- ✔ two streamers of a fourth color
- ✔ one streamer of a fifth color
- ✔ five different pen colors for each child
- ✔ photocopy of Streamers Problem Activity Sheet (pages 118–119) for each child

Preparation

None except to cut the streamers to equal lengths if necessary.

Procedure

1. This activity should be done as a group of six. Ask the class how many streamers you would need to connect one child to the other five children. Give that child five streamers of one color, with the other five children each holding the other end of one of these streamers to illustrate the answer: five.

2. Now ask the class how many streamers it would take to join another child to the remaining children to which that child is not connected (four children and four streamers). Use a new color for these four streamers to illustrate this relationship.

3. Continue the same process, with a new color of streamers each time, for the remaining children. By the time you get to the sixth child, all children should already be connected by streamers: five of one color, four of another color, three of a third color, two of a fourth color, and one of a fifth color. The colors themselves will lead the children to see the additive solution immediately. Questions such as "How many kids are there?" "How many streamers does each have to hold?" and "How many in all is that?" will point to the more general (multiplicative) solution. The multiplicative solution is more general because it works with any number just as easily.

4. After introducing the children to the concept using the streamers, have them try out the same problem on their activity sheets, where the dots represent children and the lines are streamers.

5. For each set of dots they figure out, have them write the number of streamers in the chart on page 119. The first few are filled in to get them started. For example, one child (or dot) requires zero streamers. Two children, as we saw with the streamer exercise above, require just one streamer. Three require three

streamers. The children then try to figure out how many streamers they would need to connect four children, then five, then six. Encourage them to use different colors for the streamers that come from each dot, similar to the way you used different colors of streamers for each child when you modeled the streamers problem as a group.

6. After the children have figured out how many streamers are required to connect six children, ask them if they can see a pattern in the number of streamers and children. Can they find a general solution, a rule that will always work to find the number of streamers no matter how many children there are? When looking for a general solution, children may be tempted to look for a pattern in the numbers themselves, but because this is a more difficult pattern (a second-degree pattern), this method will be difficult. Using the worksheet, you could ask helpful questions such as "How do you know when you have counted all the lines from each dot?" and "Can you predict how many lines there will be at each dot if there are seven dots?"

7. Once they have come up with the idea of multiplying the number of children (dots) by one fewer than the number of children, it is time to check if these results match the table data. Often if they write the predicted results next to each counted result in the chart, they will see that the multiplication method counts each line twice (from both ends), and all they have to do now is divide by two.

Children need to understand the idea of multiplication before the general rule (or *formula*) will make sense. Younger children who are not comfortable with multiplying may prefer the method (for example, in the six-dot case) of coloring the first five lines in one color, then the next four lines in another color, and so forth, ultimately adding up the numbers from n – 1 (when n = 6) to 1: 5 + 4 + 3 + 2 + 1 = 15. They won't understand the multiplicative formula, of course, but they'll get a taste of the recursive pattern involved using addition instead of multiplication and division.

Suggestions

- It is amazing to see even six-year-olds catch on to the pattern that we need one fewer new streamer each time, which they will if they get one of the streamers being handed out.

- Another interesting method, which children as young as eight may discover, is to examine all the results in the chart and notice that the number of streamers increases by a number that is one bigger each time. That is, in the pattern of the number of lines 1, 3, 6, 10, 15, the difference between one number and the next keeps getting bigger by one. So the pattern of differences above is 2, 3, 4, and 5. Based on this, we would (correctly) predict that we would add 6 to 15 to get the result of 21 for the next (seven dot) case, and so on. This is a property of second-degree patterns: that the differences between numbers are predictable but not constant.

- This well-known problem is an invitation into the world of proof, with the important question being "How do we know this method will always work?" Children need plenty of time to develop an understanding of why sometimes we need to have a way to "know for sure." Looking at examples to prove something can lead to false conclusions if we don't also use reasoning. The classic case is that of concluding that all odd numbers are prime by examining 3, 5, and 7. This conclusion doesn't make the connection, through reasoning, that this doesn't apply to all odd numbers just because it happens to apply in these cases. In the streamers solution, however, the reasoning can be set up to apply to *any number of children,* each holding a number of streamers that is *one less than the number of children.* Because the argument can be seen to work for *any* number of children, we can see that it always works. This problem provides an opportunity for them to justify their reasoning, an important first step in the creation of a mathematical proof.

Assessment

Ask children to predict how many streamers it would take for a group of eight children to each be connected to every other child with a streamer.

Extension Activity

Encourage children to consider real-life situations in which the formula might apply, such as determining how many wires are necessary to set up a network of n computers, or how many meetings to set up at a conference of n people so that everyone has a chance to meet with everyone else one-on-one.

Streamers Problem
Activity Sheet

Now that you've had a chance to explore the streamers as a class, it's time to work out the same problem on paper.

1 Look at the pictures on the second page of your activity sheet and pretend each dot represents a child, and each line a streamer the children are holding. For each set of dots, solve the same problems you solved as a class using actual streamers: In each case, how many streamer pieces are needed to join every child to every other child? When you have an answer, write it in the chart on the next page. The first few are done for you as examples.

> Look for a pattern in how the numbers of streamers are increasing. If you focus on the streamers column in the chart, can you see a pattern in just that set of numbers?

2 Can you find more than one way of figuring out the number of streamers for five and six children? Think about how many children there are and how many streamers each is holding. Can you use multiplication to calculate the number of streamers if you know the number of children?

3 Can you find a rule that will always work to find the number of streamers no matter how many children there are?

> Test your rule with the actual numbers. If it doesn't work, can you fix it so it does? For example, if your rule gives you double the correct number, remember that every streamer has two ends! What can you do to correct your rule in this case?

Big Ideas for Small Mathematicians, 2007 © Zephyr Press

Streamers Problem
Activity Sheet

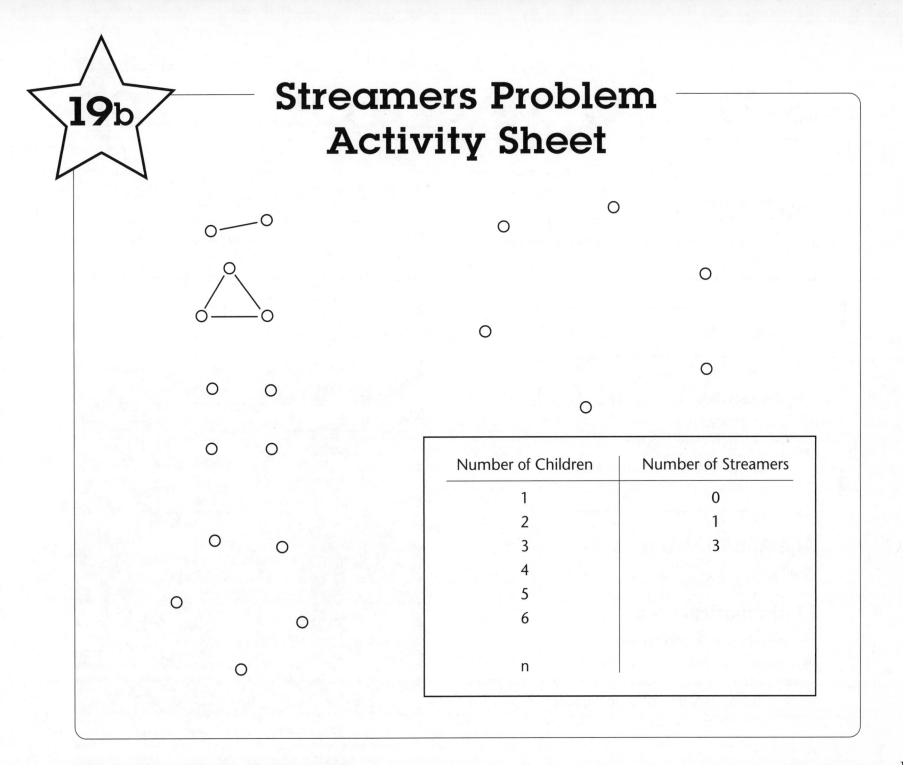

Number of Children	Number of Streamers
1	0
2	1
3	3
4	
5	
6	
n	

3-D TIC TAC TOE

The **BIG** Idea

If lines in space intersect, then a point at this intersection is on both lines. In 3-D Tic Tac Toe, this might solve two problems at once!

Content Areas in This Activity
- Three-dimensional visualization
- Intersections in space

Process Skills Used in This Activity
- Reasoning
- Problem solving

Prerequisite Knowledge and Skills
None

Age Appropriateness

Children of all ages can play this game with little support.

Mathematical Idea

Visualizing in three-dimensional space is hard to do on a two-dimensional page. In linear algebra, lines in three dimensions can be hard to picture, so why not look at them in three dimensions, instead of on the page?

This game gives practice reasoning in three dimensions, in a problem-solving context. Intersecting lines are important at various levels of mathematics, from Cartesian geometry to linear algebra, and also in this game. The use of intersecting lines leads to a trick that is an important winning strategy, namely the idea that the point of intersection of two lines is a point on both lines.

Playing the game really gets children concentrating.

HELPFUL TERMS

Algebra: *Algebra* refers to rules and language for working with mathematical symbols, such as those that stand for unknown quantities or geometric objects. *Linear algebra* is the mathematics of linear (straight-line) objects in space.

Angle: The amount of rotation needed to get from one direction to another is an *angle*. Often we speak of the angle between two lines: This is the amount of rotation needed to get from one line to the other. It is often measured in degrees.

Diagonals: The lines drawn to connect opposite corners of a quadrilateral (four-sided) figure, or the lines connecting any vertex to any other nonadjacent vertex of a figure with more than four sides, are called *diagonals*.

Linear: *Linear* refers to something that is straight, not curved, such as a straight line

Three dimensional: A *three-dimensional* object isn't flat but uses up space (volume). For example, a square is two dimensional but a cube is three dimensional.

Vertices: The point where two or more edges meet on a two- or three-dimensional shape is a *vertex*. For example, a triangle has three vertices, and a cube has eight vertices.

3-D Tic Tac Toe: Making It Work

Objectives

Children will practice problem solving and visualization in three dimensions.

Materials

- ✔ four 8" x 8" (20 cm x 20 cm) squares of Plexiglas (can be bought and cut at a building supply store)
- ✔ permanent black marker
- ✔ 12 pieces dowel, about 1½" (4 cm) each
- ✔ glue to adhere to both wood and Plexiglas, such as a hot glue gun
- ✔ 2 sets of 20 game chips
- ✔ photocopy of 3-D Tic Tac Toe Activity Sheet (on page 123) for each child

Preparation

Preparation involves constructing the three-dimensional game board as follows:

1. Score the Plexiglas squares with a marker, creating 16 small squares on each Plexiglas piece (a 4 x 4 grid)

2. Start with one square on the bottom and glue a piece of dowel vertically in each corner. When the glue is dry, add glue to the tops of the dowels and place the second square on top of these.

3. Repeat with the third and fourth square, assembling the squares in a vertical stack separated in each corner by a piece of dowel.

Chapter 20

This chip is the key to this winning set-up because it is set at two intersecting lines, one vertical and one diagonal.

Procedure

The object of the game is similar to regular tic tac toe, except the children will try to get four pieces in a straight line, and the pieces can go in any direction: vertically or horizontally, as well as diagonally in any direction. Just as in two-dimensional tic tac toe, a child can block an opponent's row with his or her own piece.

Suggestions

If children are unsure of what constitutes a straight line, have them imagine running a pencil through all four points. If an imaginary pencil sticking into the game board can touch all the pieces, then they are on the same line.

Assessment

Children are successful if they can demonstrate an understanding of the game, including blocking an opponent's line and attempting to set up straight lines of their own.

Extension Activity

Challenge the children to think about the winning strategy that involves intersecting lines. Two intersecting lines of pieces, with the point of intersection being the third chip in each, will give the player two ways to win, and the opponent can't block both.

3-D Tic Tac Toe
Activity Sheet

The object in the game is for a player to get four pieces in a straight line in any direction, similar to regular tic tac toe. You can block an opponent's row of three by putting in a piece of your own. Four in a row in any direction wins, including vertically, diagonally, and horizontally. Have fun beating the grown-ups!

FRACTALS AND INFINITY

Activity

21

The **BIG** Idea

How big or small can things get? Can patterns keep getting smaller forever?

Content Areas in This Activity

- Volume measurement
- Geometric patterning
- Numeric patterning (optional)
- Pattern rules
- Iterative patterns
- Three-dimensional visualization
- Fractal geometry

Process Skills Used in This Activity

- Reasoning (optional)
- Hypothesizing (optional)
- Problem solving (optional)
- Concept of proof (optional)
- Creativity (optional)
- Aesthetics of mathematics

Prerequisite Knowledge and Skills

None

Age Appropriateness

Fractals and infinity are great ideas that can be fairly simple or very deep. I have had discussions about these ideas with students ranging from age six to undergraduates in college!

Mathematical Idea

Dealing with infinitely small (and large) quantities has always been a major challenge for mathematicians, and it has only been in the last century or so that mathematicians have become more comfortable with these ideas.

In the last few decades, mathematicians have begun to explore a brand new area of geometry, called *fractal geometry*. This term was invented by a man named Benoit Mandelbrot, who worked in the research department at IBM and used computers to come up with amazing images—patterns that seemed to go on and on, on smaller and smaller scales. Even as you zoom in closer and closer, the shape relationships seem the same. Mandelbrot describes a fractal as something that, like a straight line, stays the same as you move closer and closer to it, but that is not a straight line. He contrasts a fractal to something like a circle, which looks less like a circle and more like a straight line as you magnify a portion of it. The Earth, for example, is not a fractal—as we get closer and closer to it, it begins to look flatter. Nature is so full of fractals, mathematicians and scientists are finding that fractal geometry is often a better way to describe nature than traditional Euclidean geometry!

In this activity, the children get just a taste of the idea of fractals and try to find fractals in the world around us. They also get to create a very basic fractal using only paper and scissors.

The extension activity introduces children to the notion of a limit, which is an important intuitive idea. In the extension activity, children are asked to imagine that the open faces of the cut-out boxes are also covered with paper to enclose the boxes. They are asked to imagine adding up the volumes of these boxes, continuing this infinitely. There is a seeming contradiction because even though a positive volume is being added with each iteration, it is hard to imagine the volumes adding up to more than the size of the classroom. The key is the notion of a limit: As long as what we are adding on each time gets closer and closer to zero by a set ratio, there will be a limit beyond which the sum will not go (although we can get as close to it as we like). When we work with infinitely small numbers, the results can be interesting!

To check if something is a fractal, think of zooming in on it and looking to see if the forms remain the same. A fern is a natural fractal: As you look closer at a frond, it seems to be composed of many tiny fronds, identical to the larger frond. These tiny fronds, in turn, seem to be composed of even tinier fronds, and so on.

Fractal Websites

- www.scienceu.com/geometry/fractals/
- http://library.thinkquest.org
- www.mathsnet.net/fractals.html
- www.Mathworld.wolfram.com/Fractal.html

HELPFUL TERMS

Euclidean geometry: This is a type of geometry of plane (flat) figures, made famous by the historical mathematician Euclid, who lived 2,300 years ago.

Fractal: The modern mathematician Benoit Mandelbrot coined this term to refer to self-similar objects. These are objects that look the same as you get closer and closer to them, with each smaller part a version of the whole, but they are not straight lines. For example, a jagged coastline looks jagged from afar, as it does if you go closer and closer—the jaggedness repeats even to the scale of grains of sand from the coastline, which look jagged under a magnifying glass. It turns out that nature is full of such objects, such as snowflakes and ferns. *Fractal geometry* is a type of mathematics for describing and constructing such objects.

Infinity: By definition this term is undefinable! We might try to define it by saying that it is a number bigger than all numbers, but since there can clearly be no such number, we have not really defined it. It exists as a theoretical construct only.

Iterative process: Repeating a rule over and over, possibly on a smaller or larger scale, is an *iterative process*. For example, take your calculator and enter 1,000 and hit the square root button again and again. This is an iterative process that gives a sequence of numbers converging to 1.

Patterns: Sets of items, such as numbers or shapes, that are continued in a predictable way are called *patterns*. Patterns created using shapes are called *geometric patterns*. *Linear patterns* change by the same amount each time: for example, 2, 4, 6, 8, . . . (changing by 2) or red, blue, red, blue. *Nonlinear patterns* change by a different amount each time: for example, 2, 4, 7, 11, 16, . . . (changing by 2, then 3, then 4, then 5, and so on) or red, blue, red, blue, blue, red, blue, blue, blue, . . . *Rotational patterns* are patterns created by rotating a shape or image. For example, a minute hand traces a rotational pattern around a clock face.

Recursive solution/recursion: The idea of getting the answer to a repeated process by knowing the previous term and how much the terms change each time is *recursion*.

Sierpinski triangle: A *Sierpinski triangle* is a pattern created in a triangle using a repeated (iterated) rule of joining the midpoints of each side to create a new triangle in the middle, then removing the new triangle (or coloring it black). See the photo on page 127, for example.

Fractals and Infinity: Making It Work

Objectives

Besides bumping into the notion of infinity, children will have a chance to appreciate the beauty of mathematics and study the wonderful patterns of fractals.

Materials

- ✔ examples of fractals (see Preparation for tips)
- ✔ magnifying glass (optional)
- ✔ 11" x 17" paper for each child
- ✔ scissors for each child
- ✔ photocopy of the Fractals and Infinity Activity Sheet (on page 130) for each child

Preparation

Gather as many fractal examples and fractal-like objects as you can to demonstrate the idea and open the discussion. You can find many beautiful fractals on the web (just search for the keyword "fractal" or try the sites listed in the box on page 125). You could also bring in a book of fractal pictures.

A comic or cereal box that has a picture in a picture in a picture would also be helpful. You could bring in any of the objects shown or mentioned throughout this activity, such as maple leaves or fern fronds, dream catchers, or a Sierpinski triangle.

The Sierpinski triangle is one example of a fractal.

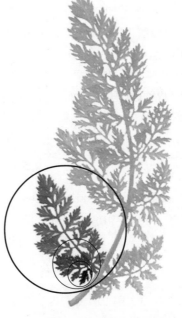

Ferns have fractal properties.

Image by Brent Davis, from *Engaging Minds: Learning and Teaching in a Complex World* (2000, p. 72), used by permission from Lawrence Erlbaum Associates, Publishers, Mahwah, NJ.

Dream catchers also have fractal patterns.

Procedure

1. Begin by discussing the idea of fractals, that they are self-similar on every level, meaning their forms repeat on smaller and smaller levels, like the fronds of a fern. Pass around the examples of fractals you've brought in and discuss them specifically. Children can investigate fractals by looking at ferns (or pictures of them), snowflakes, or maple leaves under a magnifying glass. Certain root structures also have this property. Ask the children if they can think of other fractal examples, particularly those found in nature.

☞ **The mathematical term for a repeating pattern like those found in fractals is *recursion*. Children can sense the concept of recursion by playing the following game: Tell the children that when they hear a clapping sound, they are to clap their hands. Then start the recursive pattern by clapping your hands. When they hear a clap, they clap, and so on infinitely.**

2. After the children seem to have a basic understanding of fractals, get them started on creating a basic three-dimensional fractal using a sheet of paper and scissors. Have them start by folding their paper in half vertically.

3. Have them set the folded paper in front of them, with the fold on the bottom, then make two vertical cuts about a quarter of the way in from each edge (on the right and on the left). The cuts should go halfway up the paper. See the first photo on page 129. They have now completed the fractal rule once. This rule is to fold the paper, then make two vertical cuts halfway up and a quarter-way in from each side.

4. Now they apply the rule again. Have them fold the middle piece, between the two cuts, up to line up with the top edge of the paper. Then they make two cuts, a quarter-way in from the first two cuts and halfway up the remaining paper. Then they fold the cut-out piece up to line up with the top edge of the paper, repeating the folding and cutting until they can't continue! Then have them open up the paper to see the results of the repeating pattern. If they refold the paper, they can create pop-up boxes from the fractal.

Suggestions

- If the children need more help in understanding the nature of fractals, have them draw their own picture of themselves drawing a picture of themselves, drawing a picture of themselves, and so on (or just discuss this idea).

- Shopping malls that have mirrors on two parallel walls are wonderful places to go and think about recursion and infinity. They are great places to talk about the idea of things going on and on and to think about how big infinity is.

- Unfolding the paper fractal may require some adult assistance. Half of the folds will have to be refolded in the opposite way to create the pop-up boxes. It is easiest to get the largest box popping up the right way and then work to the next smallest set, and so on.

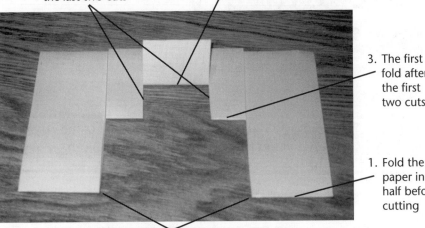

4. The second set of cuts, a quarter of the way in from the last two cuts

5. The fold after the second set of cuts

3. The first fold after the first two cuts

1. Fold the paper in half before cutting

2. The first two cuts, each a quarter-way in from the sides, going up halfway

▲
Making the three-dimensional fractal requires applying the same rule over and over: fold, cut, fold, cut, fold, cut, . . .

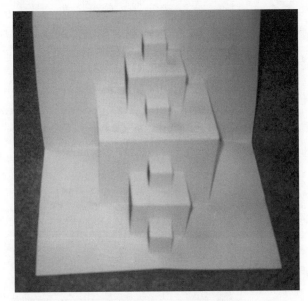

The three-dimensional fractal opened up.

Assessment

Challenge the children to create their own fractals as a way of assessing their understanding of the concept. They can try drawing fractals, creating them with scissors and paper like the one at left, or any other means they can think to try, as long as they can create and follow a fractal rule by repeating a particular pattern on smaller and smaller (or larger and larger) scales.

Extension Activity

Using the paper fractal from the activity sheet, have children imagine that the back, bottom, and sides of the boxes are covered with paper so that all boxes are enclosed. Have them discuss with a partner whether they think the volumes of all these boxes added up will keep on getting bigger and bigger. If they think so, does this mean the sum of the volumes will eventually get bigger than the classroom? Or will the sum stop somewhere? Things get interesting in mathematics when we continue processes infinitely!

Fractals and Infinity
Activity Sheet

A pattern that continues, but gets smaller and smaller (or larger and larger), and that could theoretically go on forever is a fractal pattern. Many things in nature have fractal properties, such as a fern does. You can look at the fronds of a fern and see a tiny row of fronds on the fronds. If you look at this tiny row of fronds, you'll see that these fronds have their own tiny rows of fronds, and so on.

After discussing and exploring fractals with your class, try making the simple three-dimensional fractal below.

1 Fold an 11" x 17" piece of paper in half vertically and set the paper in front of you horizontally, with the fold facing you.

2 Make two vertical cuts about a quarter of the way in from the sides and about halfway up the paper.

3 Fold the piece between the two cuts up so that it lines up with the top edge of the paper.

4 Make two more vertical cuts a quarter of the way in from your last two cuts and halfway up the rest of the paper.

5 Continue folding and cutting this way as long as you can! Can you describe the *fractal rule* for this activity? In other words, what pattern of actions are you repeating over and over?

If the paper were large enough, you could repeat this many times and the pattern would continue!

6 When you can't cut any more, open up the paper to see the three-dimensional fractal you've created. Starting with the largest box you can see in the fractal, reverse some of the folds so the box sticks out. Then move to the next box and repeat this action, and so on until all of the boxes pop up. Enjoy finding fractals all around you in your world—from maple leaves to snowflakes!

Big Ideas for Small Mathematicians, 2007 © Zephyr Press

TETRAHEDRAL FRACTAL

Activity

22

The **BIG** Idea

We can make our own three-dimensional fractal—but can we ever be done?

Content Areas in This Activity

- Volume measurement (optional)
- Geometric patterning
- Pattern rules
- Iterative patterns
- Three-dimensional visualization
- Fractal geometry

Process Skills Used in This Activity

- Hypothesizing (optional)
- Problem solving (optional)
- Aesthetics of mathematics

Prerequisite Knowledge and Skills

Activity 21 (helpful)

Age Appropriateness

Even young children can get involved in the creation of these structures. For example, a seven-year-old cut all the straws, pipe cleaners, and tissue for the small structure shown in the photograph on page 133. The first quarter section (four tetrahedrons) was assembled by an adult, and the flat faces of the other three sections were assembled by the child and finished by the adult. The child glued on all tissue paper. Older children can finish the creation independently.

The Mathematical Idea

The more mathematicians learn about fractals, the more interesting they turn out to be. Not only do they provide an interesting way to talk about things that go on forever, they are turning out to have many practical applications in science, such as the study of plant structures or human blood vessels. Many fractals are also very beautiful. (See page 125 for a list of websites that contain fractal images.) In this activity, you and the children will enjoy the beauty of a three-dimensional fractal that children can easily create. This activity also gives children a chance to practice spatial reasoning in three dimensions.

HELPFUL TERMS

Edge: An *edge* is the straight line that bounds a closed shape. For flat shapes we usually call these *sides*, but in three dimensions we call them *edges*. For example, a cube has 12 edges. Think of it as the number of toothpicks it would take to construct it, or in the case of this activity, the number of straws!

Equilateral: A figure with all sides equal (which will make the angles equal, too) is *equilateral*. We refer to a triangle with all three sides equal as an equilateral triangle. We generally call an equilateral rectangle a square, so we don't really need the term equilateral in that context. For pentagons and shapes with more sides than that, the term *regular* is generally used to imply the sides are equal.

Face: The flat outside surfaces of a three-dimensional solid are called *faces*. For example, a cube has six faces.

Fractal: The modern mathematician Benoit Mandelbrot coined this term to refer to self-similar objects. These are objects that look the same as you get closer and closer to them, with each smaller part a version of the whole, but they are not straight lines. For example, a jagged coastline looks jagged from afar, as it does if you go closer and closer—the jaggedness repeats even to the scale of grains of sand from the coastline, which look jagged under a magnifying glass. It turns out that nature is full of such objects, such as snowflakes and ferns. *Fractal geometry* is a type of mathematics for describing and constructing such objects.

Iterative process: Repeating a rule over and over, possibly on a smaller or larger scale, is an *iterative process*. For example, take your calculator and enter 1,000 and hit the square root button again and again. This is an iterative process that gives a sequence of numbers converging to 1, so we say that 1 is the *limit* of this iterative, or recursive, process.

Polyhedron: A *polyhedron* is a three-dimensional shape with polygons as faces. For example, a cube is a polyhedron with six square faces. The plural of polyhedron is *polyhedra*.

Tetrahedron: A three-dimensional shape (polyhedron) made with four triangular faces is a *tetrahedron*.

Vertices: The point where two or more edges meet on a two- or three-dimensional shape is a *vertex*. For example, a triangle has three vertices, and a cube has eight vertices.

Recall that a polyhedron made with four equilateral triangles is called a tetrahedron. The basic fractal unit in this fractal is a tetrahedron. When we put four tetrahedrons together (connecting each one at a vertex with a gap in the center) we create a new tetrahedron (see the photo below). This new tetrahedron (composed of four tetrahedrons) can be combined with three others like it to form yet another tetrahedron (see the photo on page 135). This is the iterative process that will create the fractal. This activity works very well for a large group of children as a collaborative activity.

Constructing the fractal unit.

Tetrahedral Fractal: Making It Work

Objectives

- Children will experience the self-similarity of fractals.
- Children will enjoy creating a great three-dimensional fractal pattern and get a sense of how the process could theoretically be repeated infinitely.
- Children will build teamwork skills.

Materials

- ✔ two pipe cleaners and six straws for each single tetrahedron
- ✔ 8" x 8" (20 cm x 20 cm) tissue for each face
- ✔ glue stick for each child or small group
- ✔ six twist ties (or 4", 10-cm, pieces of string) for each set of four tetrahedrons you plan to attach together
- ✔ transparent tape for each group
- ✔ photocopy of the Sierpinski triangle on page 127 (optional)
- ✔ photocopy of the Tetrahedral Fractal activity sheet (on pages 136–137) for each child

Preparation

None

Procedure

1. Have children cut six straws to about 6 inches (15 cm) long, or use the full length for a slightly larger structure.

2. Next have children cut each pipe cleaner into four 3-inch (9-cm) pieces.

3. Children then join two straws with one 3-inch pipe cleaner piece by first folding the pipe cleaner in half, dabbing glue on each end (including the folded end), then inserting the folded end into one straw, and the other two ends into a second straw.

4. They join a third straw, using two more pipe cleaner pieces, to the other two connected straws to make a triangle shape. This triangle will be the base of the tetrahedron.

☞ **The children can use transparent tape to hold joins in place until the glue dries. The glue should be allowed to dry before continuing.**

5. Next have children add one more straw at each vertex of the triangle by adding glue to another pipe cleaner piece folded in half. They then put the folded end into a new straw, then separate the two pipe cleaner ends so that they stick out. One end can go into each of the two straws at the vertex of the triangle.

6. The three just-added straws can be joined with two pipe cleaners at the top in the same way.

7. Next they cut the tissue into three triangles, which will be the sides of each face. The triangle should be 6" x 6" x 6" (or 15 cm x 15 cm x 15 cm) if using 6-inch straws.

8. Have the children apply glue along the edges of each tissue triangle before sticking them on the straws. If the tissue tears, it may be easier to put glue on the outer sides of the straws, then press the tissue on.

9. The children then repeat steps 1 through 8 three more times to create four tetrahedrons altogether. As they do, talk about the idea of patterns that keep going and get bigger and bigger in a potentially never-ending cycle. If you haven't already discussed fractals in class, introduce the term *fractal* at this point. It might be interesting to compare this fractal to the two-dimensional version, the Sierpinski triangle shown in the previous activity (page 127).

10. They attach their four tetrahedrons together, with three of them as the base and the fourth on top (as shown in the photograph on page 133). They can use twist ties (or more pipe cleaners or string) to hold or tie vertices of two tetrahedrons together. They should lift the tissue slightly to allow the twist tie to pass through the straws to hold the tetrahedrons in place.

11. After each child makes a tetrahedron as in the photo on page 133 (one fourth of the structure in the photo on page 135), then a group of four children can combine work to make the larger tetrahedral structure. They tie vertices in place, as before, to assemble the structure.

Suggestions

- Considering that the mathematical importance of the structure is its self-similarity, continue the construction process until children can see that aspect.
- Using different colors of tissue paper for each unit of four single tetrahedrons can give an interesting result.

Assessment

Children should be able to discuss the basic idea of a fractal after doing this activity (and possibly activity 21, on page 124).

Four sections like this one can be connected in the same pattern to make an even larger fractal, which can be connected to three other sections of the same pattern to make an even larger fractal, and so on!

Extension Activity

Four of these structures could then be assembled together in the same way to make a larger fractal; then four classes could meet in the gym and put their four pieces together to make a larger similar structure! This is an ideal collaborative learning experience. (If the structure will be huge, you may need to support the top vertex with a guy wire hanging from the ceiling.)

Tetrahedral Fractal
Activity Sheet

You are going to create a three-dimensional fractal that can be made nearly as big as you like. You can get lots of friends involved and create a huge structure in the gym or outside, or just make a small one for the table. We'll start small.

The basic unit of this fractal is a three-dimensional shape called a *tetrahedron,* made of four equilateral triangles. So it has four faces, four vertices, and six edges. The edges will be made of straws, and the vertices made with pipe cleaners. Then the top faces are covered with tissue paper.

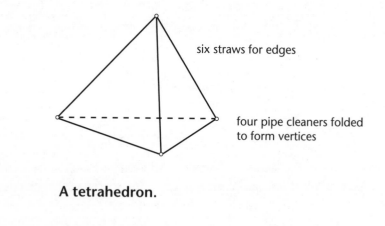

six straws for edges

four pipe cleaners folded
to form vertices

A tetrahedron.

1 First cut six straws to the same length, about 6 inches (15 cm) long.

2 Cut each pipe cleaner into four 3-inch (9-cm) pieces.

3 Fold one piece of pipe cleaner in half, dab glue on each end (including the folded end), and insert the folded end into one straw, and the other two ends into another straw.

4 Fold another piece of pipe cleaner, dab glue on each end, and stick the folded end into one of the two connected straws. Attach one more straw to the other end. Now shape the straws into a triangle, and secure the third join with another pipe cleaner piece as before.

5 Now prepare three more straws and pipe cleaners by folding one pipe cleaner piece in half, putting glue on each end, and inserting the folded end into the new straw. Separate the two pipe cleaner ends sticking out and insert one into each straw at the vertex of your existing triangle. Do this for each vertex of your triangle.

Tetrahedral Fractal Activity Sheet

6 Now join the loose ends of the three new straws together in a similar way, using two more pipe cleaner pieces to form the top vertex of the tetrahedron. Let the glue dry before continuing. Use transparent tape to secure the joins until the glue dries.

7 Cut the tissue into three triangles to cover the top three faces of the tetrahedron.

8 Apply glue along the edges of each tissue triangle before sticking them on the straws, or put glue directly on the straws and press the tissue on.

9 Repeat steps 1 through 8 three more times to create four tetrahedrons altogether.

10 Attach your four tetrahedrons so that you have three connected as a base and a fourth resting on top of the three. Use twist ties (or more pipe cleaners or string) to wrap through the straws at two vertices of two separate tetrahedrons. Lift the tissue slightly to allow the tie to pass through. Do this until all four are connected.

11 Next, get together with three other children to connect your tetrahedron structures together, using twist ties or pipe cleaners, into an even larger structure. This process can be repeated as many times as space or time permits. Have fun working on this one with as many friends as you can find!

Big Ideas for Small Mathematicians, 2007 © Zephyr Press

Glossary

algebra: *Algebra* refers to rules and language for working with mathematical symbols, such as those that stand for unknown quantities or geometric objects.

angle: The amount of rotation needed to get from one direction to another is an *angle*. Often we speak of the angle between two lines: This is the amount of rotation needed to get from one line to the other. It is often measured in degrees. (See also *degree*.)

area: *Area* is the number of 1 x 1 squares that it takes to cover a surface. For example, the area of a 2-inch by 3-inch rectangle is 6 square inches (that is, 2 x 3 = 6); in other words, it takes six 1-inch by 1-inch squares to cover it.

base: The number of symbols in a number system is its *base*. For example, in base 10 we use the symbols 0, 1, 2, 3, . . . 9, and after 9 we start again at 0 in the ones column and *regroup* the one to the next column (tens), giving 10. Base 10 came about because we have 10 fingers, so it is convenient. If we had only 6 fingers, maybe our number system would look like this: 0, 1, 2, 3, 4, 5, 10, 11, 12, 13, 14, 15, 20, 21 . . . These numbers are in base 6. The number 21 in base 6 means 2 x 6 + 1, or 13 in base 10.

carrying: An old-fashioned term for regrouping (see *regrouping*).

circumference: The perimeter of, or distance around, a circle is called its *circumference*.

composite number: A number that has whole number factors is a *composite number*; in other words, it has numbers that divide into it with zero remainder other than 1 and itself. Numbers that do not have such factors are prime (see *prime number*). For example, 6 is composite because it can be divided by 2 and 3, with zero remainder. *Note:* By convention, 1 is considered to be neither prime nor composite.

conservation of area: This term refers to the idea that if you arrange sections of an area differently, the total area (the sum of the areas of the pieces) remains the same.

cube: A three-dimensional object with six square faces is a *cube*. All the angles are 90 degrees.

degree: A unit for measuring rotation, abbreviated as °, is a *degree*. A complete rotation is said to be 360 degrees. This comes from the historical thought that it took 360 days for the Earth to revolve once around the sun. Two lines at right angles form angles of ¼ rotation, which is 90 degrees (that is, 360 divided by 4).

diagonals: The lines drawn to connect opposite corners of a quadrilateral (four-sided) figure, or the lines connecting any vertex to any other nonadjacent vertex of a figure with more than four sides, are called *diagonals*.

diameter: The distance across a circle, through the center, is called the *diameter.*

divisibility: The *divisibility* of a number describes whether any numbers can be divided into it with no remainder. For example, 10, 15, and 20 are divisible by 5. The divisibility rule for 5 is that 5 will divide evenly (with no remainder) into numbers that end in 5 or 0. (See also *factors.*)

edge: An *edge* is the straight line that bounds a closed shape. For flat shapes, we usually call these *sides,* but in three dimensions we call them edges. For example, a cube has 12 edges—think of it as the number of toothpicks it would take to construct it.

equation: A mathematical statement with an equals sign that shows that two quantities have the same measure is called an *equation.* It may include unknown quantities. For example, 9 + 1 = 2 x 5 is an equation, and so is 2x = 10.

equilateral: A figure with all sides equal (which will make the angles equal, too) is *equilateral.* We refer to a triangle with all three sides equal as an equilateral triangle. We generally call an equilateral rectangle a square, so we don't really need the term equilateral in that context. For pentagons and shapes with more sides than that, the term *regular* is generally used to imply the sides are equal.

Euclidean geometry: This is a type of geometry of plane (flat) figures, made famous by the historical mathematician Euclid, who lived 2,300 years ago.

even and odd numbers: *Even numbers* are divisible by 2, and *odd numbers* are not. Two people can share an even number of objects, but an odd number of objects will have one object left over.

face: The flat outside surfaces of a three-dimensional solid are *faces.* For example, the prism drawn at the right has five faces, two of them triangles and three of them rectangles.

factors: Numbers that divide evenly (with no remainder) into a number are *factors* of that number. (See also *divisibility.*)

Fermat's last theorem: *Fermat's last theorem* is a result put forth by French mathematician Pierre de Fermat several hundred years ago. He observed that there are lots of examples in which the sum of two squares is a square (e.g., $3^2 + 4^2 = 5^2$) but that this can never happen for whole numbers to powers greater than 2. For example, it's never true that the sum of two cubes is a cube, when the cubes have whole-numbered sides. So $3^3 + 4^3$ does not equal 5^3 or 6^3 or cubes of any other whole numbers.

formula: An algebraic rule for getting a result is a *formula.* For example, the formula for the area of a rectangle is length x width = area.

fractal: The modern mathematician Benoit Mandelbrot coined this term to refer to self-similar objects. These are objects that look the same as you get closer and closer to them, with each smaller part a version of the whole, but they are not straight lines. For example, a jagged coastline looks jagged from afar, as it does if you go closer and closer—the jaggedness repeats even to the scale of grains of sand from the coastline, which look jagged under a magnifying glass. It turns out that nature is full of such objects, such as snowflakes and ferns. *Fractal geometry* is a type of mathematics for describing and constructing such objects.

fractions: *Fractions* are pieces into which a whole can be divided. If A has ¹/₂ of a pizza and B has ¹/₃ of the pizza, then C has the remaining ¹/₆; these three fractions make up the whole.

Gauss's formula: *Gauss's formula* is one he invented when asked by a teacher to add up the numbers 1 to 100 as a punishment. He added them up twice like this:

$$1 \quad + \quad 2 \quad + \quad 3 \quad + \quad 4 \ldots + \quad 100$$
$$100 \quad + \quad 99 \quad + \quad 98 \quad + \quad 97 \ldots + \quad 1$$

and saw that for twice the sum he had 100 pairs of sums of 101. So he calculated the sum as 100 x 101 ÷ 2. In general, the formula for the sum of numbers 1 to n is n (n + 1) ÷ 2.

geometry/geometric: These terms refer to the mathematics of shapes, in both two and three dimensions. (See also *Euclidean geometry* and *fractal*.)

height: The vertical measure of an object, measured from the base to the highest point, is its *height*.

hexagon: A shape with six sides is a *hexagon*. A regular hexagon is a shape with six equal sides.

hypotenuse: This term specifically refers to the side of a right-angled triangle that is opposite the right angle—it will be the longest side of the triangle.

hypothesize: Another name for *hypothesize* is *conjecture*. It means to put forth an unproven theory for testing.

infinity: By definition this term is undefinable! We might try to define it by saying that it is a number bigger than all numbers, but since there can clearly be no such number, we have not really defined it. It exists as a theoretical construct only.

iterative process: Repeating a rule over and over, possibly on a smaller or larger scale, is an *iterative process*. For example, take your calculator and enter 1,000 and hit the square root button again and again. This is an iterative process that gives a sequence of numbers converging to 1, so we say that 1 is the *limit* of this iterative, or recursive, process.

Klein bottle: A *Klein bottle* is an imaginary mathematical object that is a three-dimensional bottle with a handle that twists into the fourth dimension and goes back inside the bottle. So it is a bottle with one surface—no inside or outside. (See also *topology* and *Moebius strip*.)

length: *Length* is the measure of one dimension of a geometric object, such as one side of a rectangle.

level: *Level* means flat or parallel to the floor, as in a balanced, or equally weighted, scale.

linear: The term *linear* refers to a straight, not curved, line. A *linear equation* is an equation whose graph is a straight line.

linear patterns: See *patterns*.

measurement: A way of counting or quantifying distance or area, using a particular unit, is *measurement*.

Moebius strip: A *Moebius strip* is a strip of paper (a two-dimensional object) with a twist in the third dimension that enables the back to meet the front so it has just one side. (See also *topology* and *Klein bottle*.)

net: A layout of flat faces that fold up into a particular three-dimensional object is called a *net*. For example, you can arrange six squares into a number of nets that will fold up to construct a cube.

nonlinear patterns: See *patterns*.

one dimensional: A straight-line path is *one dimensional*. The straight-line distance to another spot is a one-dimensional measurement.

parallelogram: A four-sided (quadrilateral) shape that has parallel opposite sides is a *parallelogram*. Opposite sides are also equal. A rectangle is a special parallelogram in which the angles are 90 degrees.

patterns: Groups of items, such as numbers or shapes, that are continued in a predictable way are called *patterns*. Patterns created using shapes are called *geometric patterns*. *Linear patterns* change by the same amount each time: for example, 2, 4, 6, 8, . . . (changing by 2) or red, blue, red, blue. *Nonlinear patterns* change by a different amount each time: for example, 2, 4, 7, 11, 16, . . . (changing by 2, then 3, then 4, then 5, and so on) or red, blue, red, blue, blue, red, blue, blue, blue, . . . *Rotational patterns* are patterns created by rotating a shape or image. For example, a minute hand traces a rotational pattern around a clock face. *Second-degree patterns* are nonlinear patterns that have a second-degree term in them, such as n^2.

pentagon: A flat geometric shape (polygon) with five sides is a *pentagon*.

pi: This is the name for a special number (3.14159 . . .), written using the Greek letter π, that is the number of times you have to multiply the diameter of a circle to get the circumference. Pi's decimal expansion goes on forever.

place value: *Place value* refers to the idea that a digit's column affects its value. For example, a 2 in the ones column means 2, but a 2 in the hundreds column means 200.

plane: A flat, or *two-dimensional*, surface is called a *plane*.

polygon: A flat (two-dimensional) shape with straight sides is a *polygon*. For example, a hexagon is a polygon with six sides.

polyhedron: A *polyhedron* is a three-dimensional shape with polygons as faces. For example, a cube is a polyhedron with six square faces. The plural of polyhedron is *polyhedra*.

prime number: A number that has no factors other than itself and 1 is a *prime number*. That is, it can't be divided evenly (with no remainder) by numbers other than itself and 1. For example, 5 is prime because 5 = 1 x 5 only, but 6 is not prime because 6 = 2 x 3 as well as 1 x 6.

probability: The branch of mathematics that has to do with predicting the likelihood of events is called *probability*. For example, when we roll a die, the probability of rolling a 6 on a single roll is ¹⁄₆. There are six possibilities, all equally likely, so each will come up one sixth of the time.

product: The result we get when multiplying two or more numbers is called a *product*. For example, multiplying 2 times 3 gives a product of 6.

proof: A mathematical *proof* is a sequence of logical deductions to establish the truth of something new from something we know. If the proof applies to an idea that includes an infinite number of values, then examples are not enough to prove something. More recently, arguments that show an idea by moving through the range of possibilities (say, with a diagram on a computer) are being considered as close to mathematical proofs, often dubbed *dynamic proofs*.

proof by counter example: One accepted way to prove something false is to come up with a counter example—an example for which the idea doesn't hold. This is considered enough evidence to assert that the idea doesn't always work, so it is not universally true.

Pythagorean theorem: This theorem describes the relationship of squares drawn on each of the three sides of a right-angled triangle: The areas of the two smaller squares added together will always exactly equal the square drawn on the longer side (called the *hypotenuse*).

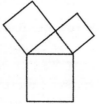

recursive solution/recursion: The idea of getting the answer to a repeated process by knowing the previous term and how much the terms change each time is *recursion*. For example, if you know a set of numbers goes up by 3 each time, and the previous number is 11, then the next number is 11 + 3, or 14.

reflection: Literally, a *reflection* is what you see when you look in a mirror, or the "mirror image" of something. In transformational geometry, reflection involves flipping an object, often to see if it looks the same (or the opposite) when flipped.

regrouping: A more modern, more accurate term for carrying is *regrouping*, which means moving groups of 10 numbers from one column into the next larger column. So if a list of numbers adds up to 14 in the ones column, we write the 4 in the ones column, regroup the 10 to a 1 in the tens column, and add it there. The same applies to all columns.

regular and irregular: In polygons, a *regular* polygon means one with sides of equal length. So a square is a regular polygon, but a rectangle is not (unless it is a square rectangle). Stop signs (like the one drawn at the right) are generally regular octagons. An *irregular* polygon is one with sides of unequal length.

rotation: When you move (or turn) an object in a circular path around a point called the center, you are *rotating* the object. For example, the tip of a clock hand rotates around the center of the clock; it follows a *rotational pattern*.

rotational pattern: See *patterns*.

rotational symmetry: *Rotational symmetry* describes a design that repeats itself as we trace out the rotation and is the same every fixed amount.

sample space: In probability, the list of all underlying possibilities, often with equal probability of occurring, is called a *sample space* (not to be confused with the *outcomes* of an experiment). For example, if we roll two dice, and the outcome is the sum of the two faces, then there are 36 possible points in the sample space, all equally likely (with probability $^1/_{36}$), but there are 11 possible outcomes (the numbers from 2 to 12). The probability of each outcome is calculated with reference to the sample space. For example, the probability of a 4 is $^3/_{36} = ^1/_{12}$.

second-degree patterns: See *patterns*.

Sierpinski triangle: A *Sierpinski triangle* is a pattern created in a triangle using a repeated (iterated) rule of joining the midpoints of each side to create a new triangle in the middle, then removing the new triangle (or coloring it black).

soma cube: A 3 x 3 x 3 cube constructed from seven different shapes made out of four or fewer cubes is a *soma cube*.

spatial reasoning: The ability to visualize in all dimensions is called *spatial reasoning*. Three-dimensional visualization is one form of spatial reasoning.

square: A polygon (that is, a flat shape) with four equal sides is called a *square*.

square numbers: *Square numbers* represent the areas of squares that have sides of whole (not fractional) numbers. For example, 25 is a square number because it is the area of a 5 x 5 square.

sum: *Sum* is a name for the number you get when you add two or more numbers. For example, the sum of 2 + 5 + 1 is equal to 8.

symmetrical: A design with parts that are the same on both sides is a *symmetrical* design: For example, by reflecting, we can create a design with two halves that are mirror images of each other.

tessellation: A geometric pattern created by repeating a shape that can completely cover a surface forever is called a *tessellation*. A tiled floor is a simple tessellation.

tetrahedron: A three-dimensional shape (polyhedron) made with four triangular faces is a *tetrahedron*.

theorem: *Theorem* is a name for a mathematical idea that can be proven always to be true.

three dimensional: A *three-dimensional* object isn't flat but uses up space (volume). For example, a square is two dimensional but a cube is three dimensional.

topology: A branch of mathematics that deals with surfaces and holes in the surfaces is called *topology*. Objects such as a doughnut and a cup are considered topologically similar because they have the same number of holes.

transformational geometry: This term refers to the geometry of moving shapes around. For example, translations (slides), rotations (turns), and reflections (flips) are movements that are possible in *transformational geometry*.

translation: Also known as sliding, *translation* means moving an object from one position to another in a straight-line movement.

triangle: A three-sided flat (plane) figure (or polygon) is called a *triangle*.

two dimensional: A flat shape (you could draw it on a piece of paper), or a shape with no thickness, is *two dimensional*.

vertices: The point where two or more edges meet on a two- or three-dimensional shape is a *vertex*. For example, a triangle has three vertices, and a cube has eight vertices.

volume: The space used by a three-dimensional shape, or the quantity of material needed to fill it, is that shape's *volume*.

wedge: A pie-shaped fraction of a circle is called a *wedge*.

whole numbers: Numbers, such as 0, 1, 2, 3, and so forth, that do not have decimal places (other than zero) are *whole numbers*.

width: The distance across a shape is its *width*.

Index

About the Author

The materials in this book have been used in Ann's *Kindermath Enrichment Project* as well as in her regular classroom, and in courses and workshops presented to many preservice and in-service teachers. Ann has taught mathematics at the elementary, secondary, and post-secondary levels, and is currently teaching preservice teacher candidates at Lakehehad University in Thunder Bay, Canada. Her research interests include the development of deeper conceptual mathematical understanding in teachers, as well as helping them to understand what learning through problem solving and investigation really means.

Big Ideas for Growing Mathematicians

Big Ideas for Growing Mathematicians

Exploring Elementary Math with
20 Ready-to-Go Activities

Ann Kajander

GRADES 5–8

Big Ideas for Growing Mathematicians, the second Big Ideas book, covers more advanced concepts, with projects including "One in a Million," where children use grains of rice to model the probability of astronomical odds; "Triangular Tessellations," in which students investigate the geometry and variations created by repeating patterns; and "Fractions of Salaries," where kids use a real-world scenario to multiply and divide fractions.

ISBN-13: 9781569762127
ISBN-10: 1569762120
128 pages, 11 × 8½
Paper, $19.95 (CAN $24.95)